THE NEW REFORMATION SERIES

# A MAN FOR US
# AND
# A GOD FOR US

### F. GERALD DOWNING

LONDON

EPWORTH PRESS

First published in 1968
by Epworth Press

*Book Steward*
Frank H. Cumbers

© F. GERALD DOWNING 1968

7162   0000   7

PRINTED IN GREAT BRITAIN BY JOHN WRIGHT AND SONS LTD.,
AT THE STONEBRIDGE PRESS, BRISTOL

# The New Reformation Series

THE past few years have seen a theological ferment which some think could herald a new Reformation. Whether it will do so it is impossible to tell; in any case it is dangerous to draw historical parallels.

Yet over the last two centuries there has been a new Renaissance, a cultural revolution, which dwarfs the old. And the danger is that, in all the excitement and our desire to do something, we may be influenced more by the fashions of the age than by fidelity to truth. Christians may be tempted to count the advance of the Gospel in headlines rather than in men and women set free for living, and to substitute journalism and TV debate for the exploration of ultimate questions in the light of the new knowledge we have gained.

At the same time, theology must not be confined to the schools, and there is no more satisfactory feature of the present situation than the interchange between professionals and non-experts which paperback publishing has facilitated. After all, it is often the man or woman in the street, the office, the factory, or the laboratory who asks the questions. The attempts to answer must not be whispered in the polysyllables of common rooms or the jargon of seminars.

It is the aim of this series to dig deep into the foundations both of Christianity and of life, but to bring what is discovered to the surface in a form which can be seen clearly and understood by anyone who is sensitive to the problems of our time and is willing to exercise his mind on them and on the possibility that the Christian tradition has something relevant to say. The books will not be too lengthy and they will avoid footnotes, critical apparatus and too much technicality. The authors have been chosen because they are scholars and experts in the subjects assigned to them but also because they are alive to the contemporary world and concerned about communication.

The method will be to look for truth about the nature of the universe and of human life and personality by seeking a fruitful and illuminating interplay between modern questions and insights and traditional Christian assertions and understandings. There is no intention to seek simply a restatement of Christianity in terms 'acceptable to modern man'. The Editors believe that it is as misguided to suggest that the truth of Christianity depends on what modern man can accept as it is simply to reiterate the ancient formulations of orthodoxy. The vital questions are 'How may we be led to see what is true?'; 'What is the nature of theological truth and how is it related to other kinds?'; 'What resources have we for understanding and meeting the real needs of men?'; 'How does Christianity look in the light of our answers to these questions and how does Christianity contribute to these answers?'

We hope that this series may be a modest contribution towards *aggiornamento* if not reformation.

# Contents

# Acknowledgements

THIS is just to acknowledge some debts and render thanks: to writers quoted in the text and notes (and to their publishers; and especially to SCM Press Ltd., for quotations from David Jenkins' *The Glory of Man*, and to Geoffrey Bles, for quotations from Lord Eccles' *Half-way to Faith*); to the Rev'd David Jenkins, and the other editors of this series, and to the Epworth Press, for the opportunity to work out the themes of this book; to Mrs. Sylvia Pelham for deciphering my type and hand writing; to many people, fellow Christians and not, and especially here in Unsworth, Bury, with whom I have talked and to whom I hope I have listened over the last few years; and especially to my wife Diana and to our children from whom I steal time. The book is dedicated in its title.

Unsworth Vicarage,
  Bury,
    Lancashire,

*September* 1967             F. G. D.

# Introduction

THIS book is one of many current attempts to answer the question, 'What is Christ for us today?' In this form it was posed by Dietrich Bonhoeffer; but it is not peculiarly his. It has always been at the back of the minds of Christian people, and often in the thoughts of non-Christians. Today it is asked much more self-consciously. We are more aware of the extent to which any question is 'our' question, and so are freer to choose the questions that we really want to ask where an earlier age might have found the 'for us' presumptuous. We can then quite boldy ask 'What is Christ *for us* today?'

In the first chapter I point out what a variety both of pictures of Jesus and of reactions to the pictures of Jesus there are. But I try to show how important it is for us to go on asking.

Next I consider the sorts of questions we today find ourselves asking of any important theme that is placed before us: 'What are the facts?' and 'Does it work? and how? and how well?' I look at some of the psychological and social factors that are involved in our attitudes to Christ, and try to show how types of approach tend to link up with the various lines adopted in the early 'classical' discussions of Christ (the discussions out of which long-accepted dogmas came).

Our questions make necessary a critical approach to the records that point us to Jesus. It is not possible in this book even to outline a critical method; that I mean to do in another book which I hope to publish in a year or so. But in the third chapter I offer a 'character sketch' of Jesus, based on current critical work: Jesus the unauthorized rabbi of Nazareth.

This and the next chapter are the heart of the book (and if you are browsing to see if it is worth your time, then I suggest you look here first). Traditional theology has said that Jesus is both God and Man: 'Therefore, following the holy Fathers, we all with one accord teach men to acknowledge one and the same Son, our Lord Jesus Christ, at once complete in Godhead and complete in manhood, truly God and truly man, consisting also of a reasonable soul and body; of one substance with the Father as regards his Godhead, and at the same time of one substance with us as regards his manhood; like us in all respects, apart from sin; as regards his Godhead, begotten of the Father before the ages, but yet as regards his manhood begotten, for us men and for our salvation, of Mary the Virgin, the God-bearer; one and the same Christ, Son, Lord, Only-begotten, recognized IN TWO NATURES, WITHOUT CONFUSION, WITHOUT CHANGE, WITHOUT DIVISION, WITHOUT SEPARATION; the distinction of natures being in no way annulled by the union, but rather the characteristics of each nature being preserved and coming together to form one person and subsistence. . . .'[1]

Popular devotion and faith have treated Jesus as God made man with less technical reserve. I try to show that all this does *not* have to be scrapped, but can provide us with a lot of help towards answering our faithfully critical questions.

Chapter 5 is probably the most technical in the book, and it is a defence of the approach that I elaborate: a defence against the attacks of a sceptical philosophy which attracts me, and against dogmatic orthodoxies that seem to imprison where they seek to guard the life that draws me. What Christians have to say (and sometimes especially what various 'new theologians' have to say) can seem woolly, useless, and even nonsense compared with the precise and practical pronouncements of all sorts of scientists. Yet when the scientists and 'their' philosophers are self-critical, attempts to express Christian faith do not suffer too badly by comparison; and I try to show how my way fits in. But there is no 'proving', and no clear certainty. Others may be able to offer proofs and certainty; I do not find I am able to. (If you do not feel the need for this defence, if it feels like someone else's argument, not yours, then pass over it. The book's positive points are mostly elsewhere.)

The last two chapters try to spell out the ways that this understanding of Jesus the Christ can affect our day-to-day living in big and little matters; they try to point to places where the words written here may perhaps become more than just words, for us.

Right at the end are notes. If a paragraph has a note in ordinary figures, that means other reading is suggested. If it has bolder figures, that means that a little more is added, to defend or elaborate what is being said. But the book is supposed to make sense without the notes.

# 1. Which Man?

## (i) A different man with the same name

IT IS all very well talking (as many current Christian writers do) about Jesus as 'the man for others'; when you get down to it, there seems to be a different man for each of them. Maybe it is not quite as bad as that. But 'the man' looks like disappearing. You need to check you know something about the identity of the man you are interested in.

Take the view of someone who spent a lot of his life interpreting the British to themselves – very successfully. Lord Beaverbrook wrote of Jesus, 'His desire was to spread happiness, not to sour life. The Sermon on the Mount is the most cheerful sermon ever preached. If the Churches have chosen to distort the Mission of Jesus by narrowing its import that is their mistake.'[1]

Then compare that picture with one drawn by the novelist D. H. Lawrence in 'The Man Who Died'. Lawrence has Jesus resuscitated from a coma in the coldness of the tomb. He escapes, and is nursed back to health by a peasant couple. He is enormously penitent for what he has done: 'death has saved me from my own salvation.' Later he finds a life that he can recognize as real, making love with a priestess of Isis.[2]

The attempts of many other writers to compose a 'Life of Jesus' were torn to pieces by Albert Schweitzer in a book he wrote at the turn of the century, before his fresh career as the remarkable and slightly eccentric doctor of Lambaréné. The English translation of his book was called *The Quest of the Historical Jesus*. The point he made painstakingly is summed up in the rather cruel remark of George Tyrrell: 'The Christ that Harnack [standing for nineteenth-century critical scholarship] sees, looking back through nineteen centuries of Catholic darkness, is only the reflection of a Liberal Protestant face, seen at the bottom of a deep well.'[3]

Look at the 'Theology' or 'Religion' section of any second-hand bookshop; or the new books in a university bookseller's; or in your local library – and you will see how great the variety is. Jesus as the rather 'commonplace Rabbi'; as the daring visionary; as the creation of the imagination of an artisan community in Rome, or a religious community in Palestine; preacher of inexpensive good-naturedness; God playing a human role; political agitator, pacific or militant; dying to save mankind or just his own integrity; purely Jewish, or the meeting point of a hotch-potch of theosophical ideas; vitally important, or not very interesting.[4]

But the question of Jesus is a real one for many people. Lord Eccles, in his *Half-way to Faith*, quotes a friend as saying: ' "We argued quite a lot about Christ but never a word about God, and Christ without God is very easily bracketed with Plato or Shakespeare or D. H. Lawrence." We thought it only honest to treat Christ's life and teaching within a strictly human framework.'[5] And a modern theologian, Günther Bornkamm, firmly agrees, from a standpoint of faith:

> How could faith of all things be content with mere tradition, even though it be that contained in the Gospels? It must break through it and seek behind it. . . . It cannot be seriously maintained that the Gospels and their tradition do not allow enquiry after the historical Jesus. Not only do they allow, they demand this effort.[6]

The situation is very confusing. I hope that some of the confusion will disappear with the help of the following pages. But I do not promise that it all will; all I do hope is to offer you a method of approach, a way of receiving as much as you can from people who have, before us, concerned themselves with Jesus. I shall rarely refer directly back to these illustrations of the kaleidoscopic divergences that exist: but they represent some of the currents in the eddying centre of the situation from which I write. They all matter to me. For the moment I quote with qualified but genuine approval once more from Lord Eccles:

> If Jesus is to be taken seriously as a guide to action – the pattern for my conscience – I have to choose between two portraits, that of the gospels and that of the Church, and I have no means of deciding between them except by intuition. . . . I find reality in the gospels and illusion in the Church. But this can only be a personal opinion. No judgement based on artistic values can be imposed on anyone else. As always each man makes his truth his own. Jesus was original precisely because he believed that truth could only be discovered by each man for himself, and that a man could assure himself of the truth about right and wrong provided – and the proviso is inescapable – he looked at other men and women as Jesus, his Lord, looked at them. Jesus offered, not a map, but eyes with which to see, knowing that light and sight are the most desirable of all gifts in all circumstances.
> Christ relies, not on our sense of duty, but on our imagination; we are not threatened but captivated into obedience.[7]

3

# (ii) Us and our world

You take your choice. You take your choice, and pay with your life. At least, Jesus seems to have said that those are the terms.

That really makes it very odd (if there is any truth in Jesus' claim). If it is a matter of life or death, and you are faced with an identification parade, you do not expect to be told just to choose. You are not electing a candidate, you are deciding a matter of fact. Is this really the man who did the deeds? Is this the real Jesus, the man who lived and walked and loved and died?

It is a question of fact, a question of what really happened. But the trouble is that it is that and more. The question of Jesus involves, for everyone who asks it, more than just a question of fact or facts. That is why it is really so easy to make a list of very different answers.

For a great many people, Jesus represents an ideal – maybe more than an ideal, but at least an ideal. They feel that he has taught them their ideals to guide their behaviour; they are sure that he has lived out those ideals in his own life. But people can lay claim to Jesus, and still have very different ideals; and they use their ideals for different purposes.

One man has a set of ideals that he comes pretty close to living by; he is a Communist and a Christian. Another is an industrialist, convinced as a Christian Capitalist; and he too lives by the standards he says he believes in. Both are very sincere. For both it is very important to be able to believe that their beliefs and ways of life have the seal of Jesus' approval, and the backing of Jesus' own life. Looking at them from any other standpoint, you can see that they cannot both be right (unless Jesus was a very woolly thinker; and that would still have to be proved). Each of them may seem to have taken up real parts of what Jesus said. But for the rest, one or both of them must be using 'Jesus' as a status symbol for his ideals. It is still important for lots of people to be able to say, Jesus Christ is a member of my party. It is an impressive name to head the list of patrons with. (A status symbol? or, as someone has suggested, a mascot?)

Try to tell your Christian Communist that Jesus did not command the end of private property – or try to tell your Christian Capitalist that he deliberately destroyed a whole stock of pigs. You are not just trying to prove an incidental matter of fact. You are attempting to change the ideals that a man actually lives by.

At any rate, in Europe and America a great many people find it tempting to twist Jesus' arm a bit so that he will speak for them; it is very hard to stand by and allow another to make him speak for a different point of view.

Try the test on yourself. Did Jesus tell everyone to break all ties of family and marriage, property and work, and follow him? Are you open to persuasion that he may have said that? or is your first reaction, 'No, it would mean chaos, he can't have done!'

'He can't have said something which contradicts what I believe is right' is an argument that helps powerfully to produce all the different pictures. 'He can't have told me to do something which my conscience forbids' – but people have very different contents to their consciences. 'Some part of his teaching must back up what I passionately and unshakeably believe in' – but good, sincere, and kind people believe immovably in very different causes.

This is not to say that people who use Jesus' name take no notice at all of what he himself says – the evidence is against that. But the question of Jesus is for many a question of how I should live and treat my children and spend my money. And obviously we all find it easier to change Jesus than to let him change us.

And further, not everyone who has some picture of Jesus or of his teaching as an ideal would really claim to live by the ideal. In fact many of us have two sets of ideals (or more). One is the back kitchen and living room and works set; and the other is the front parlour set, with the Bible and best china, which we bring out to show visitors. This is not necessarily just hypocrisy, either. No one would dream of *living* in the front room, with the front room set. It is only for scattered high points in life. No one expects you to live by your 'high' ideals. But you have them, and pass them on to your children. Maybe you really wish sometimes that you could live up to them. You wish something would happen to make you really want to. Maybe if a lot of the neighbours did, it would give you the courage to. And because there *is* always a chance that you might have to live by them, it is hard to let them be changed; even sad, if they seem to move still further away from the set you live by. It is hard to allow a change in the ideal figure that might shape your life; especially when the ideal was handed down by your mother from her mother.

But there is some hypocrisy in it, maybe a great deal. It can be a very cheap way of persuading myself that I am good. I have as good a set of high ideals, or better, than the people around, and in mint condition, never been used. And because they are 'my' beliefs, I can use them to defend myself against the world. The Jesus who gave me my neighbour to love can be used to give the seal of respectability to a self-centred intolerance and refusal to change. If I have set him to guard me against the world, I shall resist very bitterly any attempt to suborn him from my service.

This is often, and justifiably, said to be a post-Christian

6

and 'secular' age. There will be a growing number of people who do not need Jesus to stand for their ideals. They may try to look and see what he can say to them; but they will see no need to listen, if they do not like what they hear. (There is one gain: there may not be so strong an urge to make Jesus do and say just what they can approve of.) But it will still be difficult for them to look at Jesus dispassionately. He did preach his ideals; he does represent, more or less plausibly, the various ideals of many of their fellows. And towards these a man will usually find he must take some stance.

It is worth noting that there are, on the other hand, convinced Christians for whom the character and teaching of the man Jesus are not very important. I mentioned a little while back the view of Karl Barth that Jesus was a rather 'commonplace Rabbi' and Barth is not alone in holding this view. But for Barth the very insignificance of Jesus (as he sees him) is important. Jesus is the ideal man, just because he does not call attention to himself, but points you to God and allows you to be faced by the full force of God's judgement and love without any distraction. For the same sort of reason, another recent Christian writer, Paul Tillich, has talked of Jesus as one who was 'transparent' to God; and in this he has been taken up by the Anglican bishop, John Robinson, among others. And still Jesus remains an ideal because, these writers would say, this is how every man should stand before God.[8]

To talk about Jesus in Europe and America is to talk about how I or my friend or my enemy should live. It is in logic very difficult and in practice almost impossible to avoid this. And so the matter is extremely complicated.

It is in fact even more complex still. To talk about Jesus is, for many people, to talk about God. Even when they do not believe that 'God' is real, Jesus is bound up for them with the 'God' they do not believe in. And even without that, to raise the question of Jesus is to raise the question of God, because Jesus himself talked so much about God, and directed his life, or so it seems, as wholly towards his God as he was able.

When people who do believe in 'some sort of God' talk about their belief, they often say very soon something like, 'Otherwise things as a whole would not make sense.' Talk about God leads people into talk about 'things as a whole', 'how things really are, when you get to thinking deeply about them', and so on. So, even if you do not yourself go along with them, you find yourself talking about 'what is really real', about patterns, meanings, purposes for life, for the universe. And that means you are plunged into talking about much more than one life 2,000 years ago, and one other life (your own) today. To raise the question of Jesus can be to disturb or even shatter people's ways of looking at their world as well as at themselves; and so it is unlikely ever to be an easy or clear question.

We acquired our attitudes to the God we believe or disbelieve in, or our attitudes to 'things as a whole', from many different sources. We were, almost certainly, deeply affected by our parents (or parent-substitutes); they were stern, remote, vicious, loving, possessive, vacuous; united, or ready to be enlisted against each other. Some things we had already inherited from them at birth. We felt their individual and class attitudes. We shared in the patterns of activity and talk of our age group: comics, television, wireless, films, school. Whether we largely accepted or rejected these influences, consciously or sub-consciously, they are now a large part of our attitudes, important or insignificant, set or shifting, to 'things as a whole', to the 'God' we believe or disbelieve in or largely ignore. So

8

some questions, and particularly some questions of Jesus and God, will seem to us unraisable – or unanswerable. And others will so little touch us that we will be hard put to it to agree or disagree; to see that there is a question at issue at all. Others, again, may worry us all our lives.[9]

There is a further point that it would be misleading not to note. We have considered raising for ourselves questions of Jesus and of God, and have seen that these may involve deep questions about ourselves and our world(s). While a believer might allow this way of talking, he would very likely insist that it is God who acts first to present us with the answer of Jesus, and this answer throws us in question (and our world). And there are others, for instance, for whom Jesus disposes of the problem of God, by being himself the entire answer that puts us in question. The argument will return to these and other possibilities. If one of these is the interim or final standpoint that you reach, it will obviously be for you the 'correct' perspective, so that any other view must be judged to be more or less distorted. (You might even hold that to start from any other view-point than yours would be to guarantee a fruitless journey. However, if you did believe that, it is unlikely that you would be reading this. At least you are willing to suspend disbelief.) But meanwhile we shall continue along the lines with which we began.

# (iii) A 'New Reformation' Christology[10]

This book is part of 'The New Reformation Series'; and it is meant to deal with 'Christology'. A 'reformation' (of Churches or gambling laws) can come about through a blind dissatisfaction with present conditions ('anything would be better'). It can happen because there is a compelling

9

vision of something far better. It can come through an apparently chance embroilment in matters that seem quite unconnected. It may be a very mixed situation, in which all these, and other factors too, play a part.

In the present situation, churches are less and less well attended; clergymen find more and more of their traditional functions taken over by other, and specialist, professions. This creates a general discontent, clerical and lay, and piecemeal changes that seem to be for change's sake ('do something, somebody, even if it is only revise canon law').

Alongside this, old ways of thought have been re-explored and new ones pioneered. Exciting possibilities are suggested (even though some conflict with others). And bizarre fancies have the attraction of novelty.

Quite apart from decisions of individual members about sharing in worship or 'using' their clergyman; quite apart from the pedantries and visions of theologians; industrial change, the emergence of new nations, the East–West confrontation compel new structures and new thinking, compel not just random changes but particular innovations. This happens where the old may have seemed entirely satisfactory (on its own terms), and where no new possibilities had been suggested from within at all.

As a theologian, I have a personal stake in the second type of factor. But there is no way of judging in advance which will produce the best results (?the right results ?God's purpose). The first may be feverishly destructive, or shallow – or by trial and error may produce a magnificent fit with the total 'real' situation. The second may be wholly unreal, producing dreamy answers to a world spun entirely from a man's isolated imagination; or it may give the realistic drive and direction without which an empirical approach is lost in a nightmare of conflicting possibilities. And the third may make a Church into a sub-department of state or party; or present it with the demand and possibility for a Christ-like service. In a series called 'The New Reformation' we have to be concerned with questions and answers that come from all these points and more. If reformation happens, is happening, any or all of these may produce or be producing the changes; and must be explored and appreciated.

Then, in a book that claims to deal with 'Christology', we are dealing, fairly obviously, with ways of understanding 'the Christ'. But 'Christology' has come to be understood, more generally, as a discussion of terms such as 'Son of God', 'Word of God', as well as the very Jewish term 'Christ', 'Messiah', 'the Anointed'. It covers questions of the identity and status of Jesus before and after his death.[11]

Traditionally, it has been said that you must say what you know or believe about Jesus' status and identity before you can discuss his effect on you and the world. But the way we have begun our enquiry combines the two, necessarily. We have seen that the question of Jesus raises, almost inevitably, and for us quite certainly, questions of God, ourselves, and our world. We can only ask, 'What is he – for us?' and move between the questions, 'What is he?' and 'What effect on us does he have? What demands does he make?' To concentrate on one question, in the style of the old formal division, would be to make it impossible to answer even that. And in the earliest and largely formative periods of Christian thinking the distinction was often explicitly refused, for our type of reason.

'What is Christ for us today?' is the question as posed by Dietrich Bonhoeffer, and accepted by many for whom Bonhoeffer's thought is at least one thrust towards any 'new reformation', though he was executed two decades ago.[12]

Jesus – how far can we get back to a man who really lived?

For us – how important is this attempt, its success, failure, or refusal?

God – what place has talk of him for us in talk of Jesus?

And – does this leave us fairly satisfied with the questions we first asked, or does it drive us to abandon them, and use a fresh set?

# 2.  Who Asked?

## (i) Einstein and the engineers

EVERY Englishman, it is said, suffers from the mistaken belief that he has read Charles Darwin's *The Origin of Species*. (I do in fact know that I have not.) Certainly everyone who reads this has been affected noticeably, if unawares, by at least a vague 'Darwinism'. And along with this has gone a touch of Freud and a trace of Marx, and even the feeling of having sat as a schoolboy at the feet of Albert Einstein. ('If only I'd had a better physics master, I'd have understood him.')

And probably you also sat with Isaac Newton and with James Watt, while a beneficent Nature bombarded you with the evidence of rotten apples or steamy kettles until the next Scientific Truth became inescapable. Even more important, you served a full apprenticeship under a thousand nameless engineers, technicians, inventors, industrialists who made Science work. Explanations, as far as they went, and as far as you could grasp them, may have intrigued you.

Results, practical success; jet airliners, washing machines, television, modern surgery, antibiotics, computers, frozen peas: it is these that have really impressed you. Applied science increases my standard of living, my security, my life span. You may affect a disdain of it; but it would take a considerable scientific skill to let you avoid a wide use of its products.[1]

This is a deliberately commonplace selection of factors that will have influenced your thinking. The question of Jesus will put you in question; but your questions about Jesus will be shaped importantly, though maybe not completely, by a technical knowledge of, or at least a popular acquaintance with, all these. You will want, for instance, to know what real difference does it all make, what results can you expect? What effect does focusing attention on Jesus have, what comes out of a 'way of life' or a 'religion' that concentrates its attention on him?

Really, whether you like it or not, you will also have a supply of critical questions that will demand fairly precise answers. What are wanted are 'facts' (even where the questioner has not managed to ask critically what 'a fact' is). You will have a strong, if not very clear, impression that behind any important belief lies a host of ideas, good, bad, or indifferent, which may make the reporter see things the way he does. Things that are said about Jesus may be 'fact' – or they may be, they could be, just spun out of the hopes, fears, inner conflicts of the people who said them. Or it is some sort of mixture of both fact and fancy. Talk about Jesus, we have noted, is closely linked with talk about God; and that, said Feuerbach, is a projection from my inner self. Not just my individual personality structure, said Marx, but my economic and social position and aims produce my religion.

This is in the main only the other side of what we have

quite readily accepted, that the question of Jesus and God puts me in question. It is not always so acceptable to have to allow Marx and Freud (=the whole pattern of thinking that includes them) to put my questions of Jesus and God (and Marx's and Freud's questions of Jesus and God) in question. But the sceptical approach cannot stop with what other people have said about Jesus and God. It has to go on and question the questioner. Critical research is just as much shaped by the researcher's own individual make-up, his politics, his economic and social environment, as his material is by its reporters. And it can be just as distorted by these sorts of influence as the researcher may suspect is the case with the material before him. (It has often been felt that Freud's attitude to religious belief was very largely controlled by Freud's not very happy relationship with his own father.) Simply to know that this is possible for others does not itself necessarily set you free. It may even allow you a blinder self-assurance.

Of course, it is not necessary to be completely pessimistic. It may be precisely these powerful factors in your background that enable you to see particularly clearly and even objectively the issues involved: in this case, the issues involved in what has been said and what is said about Jesus and God.

Granted all this, the fact remains that questions of Jesus and God are at a disadvantage, at least at the start, today. History may not be complete bunk; but questions about what happened a thousand or two thousand years ago just do not seem at first sight – or at the twentieth inspection – all that important. Nothing really results from the answers offered. Corn does not grow better, surgeons' knives do not cut cleaner, presses do not roll faster. It even seems rather frivolous: see the expression on the face of the bulldozer man as he waits, impatient (even a little envious), for the archaeologist to pack away his notebook, trowel and broken pots. History may be absorbing as a hobby, and hobbies may be important as a part of life, and the historical showman is worth his keep; but he and his work still seem non-productive luxuries, even when they are concerned with Jesus and God.

And even as hobbies go, history does not compare all that well. If your hobby happens to be research into sub-atomic particles, and if you are fairly sure that your findings here are going to have no practical usefulness (some scientists do say this), you can still expect fairly definite results, you can repeat them for the unpersuaded, you can say what you believe will happen, and then see or show whether it does. Even designing imaginary sports car bodies, given four wheels, an engine and two passengers, you know what is aerodynamically functional, and the next man would produce much the same result. It is only styling for selling that allows one model to differ from the next.

But four historians seem likely to give you five impressions of what happened at Hastings or at Golgotha, and how are you to know which to follow? Sub-atomic research may give you irrelevant facts, but at least they may be agreed 'facts'; historical research seems to give a much less usable medley of quite conflicting opinions.

And when a question about Jesus turns into a question about God, when you move from the interplay of history and theology into 'pure' theology, there seems to be even less sure ground. Granted there are self-styled experts, 'theologians', they have no agreed method, no demonstrable subject matter, and more disagreement even than you might have expected when you learned their main starting point. When the only available experts disagree so widely, the ordinary man has to do it himself or give up in despair, and do without. (In modern British politics at least, 'theologian' is a term of abuse.)

Questions of Jesus and God begin with forbidding disadvantages. And yet, as a matter of agreed fact, they present themselves as questions that are hard to escape. If you are trying to understand complex European societies (in and out of Europe) and the Asian, African, and American cultures that have reacted to and against European influence (and, of course, now there is greater inter-action), then you have to raise the question of Jesus at least at some point. This is so, even if you end by refusing any answer (negative or positive) to the question of God and the question about yourself; and even if you end by deciding that the matter of Jesus is not very important alongside other matters of past fact.

You may not wish to understand the present, you may not mind if you are not able to deal with it as it has come to be and as it is. But if you do wish to understand, if you do wish your response to the present to be as nearly as possible informed and appropriate, then you will need to raise the question of Jesus: at least sometimes, and at least as one question along with others. And if you are reading this book, there is a very good chance that you already agree to raise the question, even if you might not agree to put it quite this way. You might prefer to start at some quite other point. However, this is how we have begun, and you are following so far.

## (ii) As a matter of fact

Questions about Jesus are inescapably (though not solely) questions of history: questions of his history, and of the history of those, from his own time on, who were concerned for him, or might at least have known of him, and have reported their response. Past ages may have been content to be told that this is Jesus as the Church now believes in him. Today we cannot but ask, 'Is that how Christians have always believed in him?' and 'How does that relate to a Jesus who was born, lived and died?' The past might have thrilled to some recent vision. The present must ask, 'How does that tie up with anything that really took place?'

Questions of history are complicated questions. The historian cannot tell you everything that ever happened; he does not know, and time forbids. He selects from what he thinks he knows of events and sequences that he thinks are relevant, and sets them out in words and sentences that focus on just some aspects of what his sources suggest to him took place. This is the only way to write history. It does not mean that the historian is free to invent, or bound to accept uncritically what his sources tell him. And his work is subject – an understatement – to his colleague's criticism. But he has to select and interpret.

The historian is (or should be) bound by the facts (even though, to be a historian, he has to choose which facts to relate). The facts that bind him are the same sort of facts as those with which the chemist or physicist deals. It is only that the historian has fewer of them, he is looking at them individually (rather than in groups). They often take much longer to establish, and accounts of them frequently remain insecure. He cannot arrange for more like them to take place as support for his account. But the biologist who is looking for the sequence of events in the life cycle of a particular worm and the historian who is studying a particular monarch are both asking questions about past facts, about what actually took place. And both will ask fewer questions than all the questions that could be asked. And both will find it hard to 'prove' their results in each case when king and worm are both dead and gone, even just very recently.

However hard the historian's job may be, and however disputed his results, he is trying to deal with facts, in a sense of 'the facts' that ties in closely with the sense of 'the facts' in any other area of research. That is one reason why the question of Jesus today is inescapably a question of historical research: a man today insists that if 'facts' seem to be, are said to be, at stake, he must have as many relevant ones as are available, as well demonstrated as possible. Only if he can raise the question of Jesus the man as in some sense a question of fact like other questions of fact, can he take the question of Jesus really seriously.[2]

A 'fact' in this setting means 'a statement of fact'. If you ask for 'the facts' then the man you ask will start *talking*. He may point to visible evidence, but he will 'tell' you 'the facts'. And to ask for statements of fact is to ask 'what really happened', in so far as it can possibly be known and stated. What really happened in the case of Jesus and his first followers and their belief in God? What has happened since because of these happenings, and what effect can they or do they have on us?

The historian's attempt to show what really took place is very similar to the attempt that is made in a court of law. Counsel examine witnesses and produce evidence to substantiate their interpretations of what happened, their views of 'the facts'. The judge helps twelve ordinary people to decide which view is right, or whether there is enough evidence. In a very important case the argument may continue for weeks. There may be appeals after the verdict. (This is being written in the week when Mr Justice Brabin published his critical enquiry into the trial and conviction of Timothy Evans, hanged years ago for the murder of his baby daughter.)

Where a will or deed or treaty is concerned, it may be a question of determining what happened centuries back. It may seem very odd to let someone in the seventeenth century or the twelfth decide what should happen to an important building site in the twentieth. Why should an eighteenth-century treaty determine the lives of twentieth-century inhabitants of Gibraltar? But until we do decide on some other way of ordering our lives that ignores completely the past (would that be possible?), questions about the past will be asked and disputes about it will have to be settled.

The more important the issue, the more complicated is the debate likely to be. But the complexity of the issues does not itself compel us to throw in our hand. The most important 'fact' may be that there is not enough clear evidence. Yet we are likely in an important issue to need more persuasion that this is so than we would demand in support of a positive reconstruction of a less interesting sequence.

It is alleged that the case of Jesus is a matter of life and death for us today. If we take the claim at all seriously, if we take his supposed place in our own past history at all seriously, then we must examine with enormous care the rival presentations of that case.

This book can only point to a few such presentations, and can present positively only its own. But its main aim is to persuade that the enquiry is above everything worth while; and to point to methods and to offer tentatively some results.

This procedure means that we sit in judgement on Jesus, and that could seem arrogant and objectionable. But primarily it is the rival advocates and opponents of Jesus who are to be judged. And we have already noted that to raise the question of Jesus and the facts of Jesus is also to put ourselves under judgement. For sure, Jesus seems to have warned against judging others and risking being judged. But the writer of the fourth gospel (for what his opinion is worth) is sure that to avoid judging Jesus, and so avoid coming under his judgement, is to avoid life: and still be judged. So we proceed with our enquiry, and note the risks.[3]

Declaring the verdict is distinct from presenting the facts; and pronouncing judgement is distinct again. But each arises out of the act that precedes; and each is performed in awareness of what is to follow. There are few if any 'bare facts' in this case of Jesus or in any other case. The bare facts are the irrelevant ones. The facts that matter are the 'true facts' in which each time the real question of Jesus is raised, and we are judged, and maybe freed – by him, for him – or, fair enough, from him.

## (iii) Members of the jury

It is time, then, to examine the jury – remembering that the jury is itself on trial. What are the likely reactions of at least some of its members to the case of Jesus?[4]

Martin is an ordinary man: that is, ordinary to an Anglo-Saxon. He is conscientious and hard-working, earning a fairly good wage, but only by doing lots of overtime. He is buying a house. He has a wife and two children and a small car which he bought new, cash down. He votes Conservative, as his father and mother do, though they live in a small and crumbling rented 'two up, two down'. They think well of someone who can make his way within the established rules. Martin does not spend much on personal luxuries; he saves for his family. If he has a fault,

21

it is being too strict with the children, too anxious about their schooling; and too fussy about the house for his wife's liking. He can keep going at anything for a long time, and persevere, so long as things are going reasonably well. But if they start going badly, he gets very depressed, and goes on the beer.

Martin does not have much time for 'religion'; but he does have some deeply felt and firmly held beliefs. Jesus was a good man, who gave us rules for how to live. Some of them were a bit extreme, but they don't apply to most people; and anyway, his disciples may have altered a thing or two in Jesus' teaching afterwards. Jesus acted out what his conscience told him to do; and if – *if* – you think much about him, he is a very impressive figure.

If you could get Martin to talk about 'religion' (but mostly you cannot) he would find it hard to see Jesus as anything 'more' than a man. Martin believes that there is a God, who is fairly distant and austere, keeps himself to himself; but this God can be addressed if you are in any special need, and will help. (This is Martin's own way with his neighbours.) 'God' is a good enough explanation of how things are, and Martin has not much time for sophisticated arguments against. Like any other man, Jesus may have had a bit of special help from this God in moments of stress, may even have been able to do miracles. But most of the time he was left on his own to get on with his life, and what more does a man need than that?

Strictly speaking, Martin is, of course, a 'heretic'. Christians have decided, by and large, that it is not enough to call Jesus a 'mere man'. Martin's cousin, Nesta, for instance, is on the jury too. She's like him in many ways, but her parents were more religious, and took her to church a lot when she was young. For her, Sunday worship is one of the rules (for Martin, it is not); and she teaches in Sunday

School, and thinks quite a bit. She accepts that Jesus was not just an ordinary man, because the Church teaches that he was more than that. But how can you make sense of this? Her answer goes something like this: Some people are specially good, and are specially used by God; a prophet in the Old Testament, a missionary eye-surgeon in India. God just does come particularly close to them, and they respond. He chooses them, and lets them get to know his ways, and get to know him, especially closely. These people still have a struggle to be good, and obey. It does not become easy, still less automatic, just because God has chosen them. God may have 'called' other people, but they have not responded. The ones you notice are the ones who used the will-power we were all born with, and battled through. In various ways God rewards them.

Jesus was the greatest example of this sort of person. In fact, in a real sense, he is unique, so Nesta would say. God came specially close to Jesus, had a special plan to make Jesus our perfect example: and Jesus obeyed perfectly. And that has for sure never yet happened to anyone else.

Of course this is not all that the Church tells Nesta to believe; she also has to try to make sense of the doctrine of Christ as part of the Trinity. God, she decides, stands over against his world like a father, creator, judge. But he stands alongside the people he chooses (maybe he tries to for everyone) like a brother as well. God has a way of being a Father over us; but he also has a way of being a Son alongside us (and a Spirit within us). God was with Jesus like a Son, as well as being a Father to him. And Jesus fitted in with God so closely at every point of his life, that you can really 'see' God, there 'in' Jesus. God was 'in' Jesus, in a very special and clear way. Nesta has read a book by a Scottish clergyman that tells her this is a good way of seeing it, and a way that in one form or another goes back to the early days of the Church (especially to the Christians of Antioch). And it is accepted in lots of Churches' official teaching, since a council of church leaders was held at a place called Chalcedon, in A.D. 451.

If things go reasonably well, Martin and Nesta will probably go on believing much the same. But lots of things can go wrong. Martin can take on a job that's too big for him to tackle. Either of them can get involved in an accident, or hit by the shock of a bereavement. They both believe that you make your own way in life, and your standard of living depends on what you earn in a fairly free economy, and things you cannot control so much, like health and life itself, depend on keeping on the right side of God. So if things do go wrong, at all seriously, they will see it as their fault, and feel guilty. They may manage to hide their guilty feelings from themselves most of the time, and from other people, by just doing a lot more. But one way or another, if Martin or Nesta do have a real problem that they have to take to God, it is going to be a problem of guilt. Am I so guilty? can I be forgiven? how can I be forgiven?

Should the problem become very severe, they will be cared for by a psychiatrist of some sort, all being well. But before and after, because they have a 'religious' background, they will probably try to find a religious answer. It may suddenly make sense to them that Jesus, the perfect man, suffered. Things did not go well with him. But he had no guilt, he at least did not deserve to be punished. Whose guilt can he have suffered for? For ours! This realization ('he has borne my sin') may come as a sudden shock, and Martin or Nesta will be 'converted'. Or it may come slowly.

They are not at all likely to question the basic pattern of earning a reward, or earning nothing, or earning punishment. When they get to feeling unbearably guilty, then either someone else must take the terrifying mental beating (it can have quite physical effects) or they go under.

If this problem of unbearable guilt does come up, it may start Martin or Nesta thinking again about God's part in Jesus' life. How could even a perfect man bear the guilt that I find intolerable – and the guilt of everyone else? Surely only God himself could take it; surely God must have been even closer than I thought to Jesus. God the Son and Jesus must have been the same person, the same personality. He must have been a real man, to be sure, if he was going to suffer for my real human sins. But he must really have been God, to be able to bear them, and take them away, and absorb the punishment they deserved.[5]

This, then, is how Martin and Nesta will start off thinking, if they are religious in a Christian country. And if an unmanageable problem crops up, it will involve a sense of guilt; and if they want a 'Christian' answer, it will probably be along these lines. They may feel they have to work the problem out for themselves (they are like that); but they will find lots of help if they want it, because even if they come with little assistance to this answer, they will find that lots of other Christian believers got there before them, and worked it all out before in some detail.

Of course, Tom, Dick, and Harry, who are also on the jury, do not see things like this at all; even though at first meeting you'd think they were very much like Martin and Nesta. Tom is a Marxist. Like Martin, he believes in hard work, though it is impossible to get satisfaction from it in a capitalist society where a man sells his labour, and so is alienated from what should give his life purpose and drive. In fact, being the person he is, he does enjoy working hard, and earning in a capitalist society; and this makes him guilty. So he works even harder, in his spare time, for the Party. If the Party does not prosper, it is the fault of men like him, seduced by the bosses. But he can (or could) confess to his brothers, make himself small, let himself be destroyed for his massive errors. Jesus? a workers' revolutionary, misguided; or a figment of the imagination of a depressed proletariat, captured very quickly by the ruling classes to support their position. The decision to call Jesus 'God'? merely electing him into the establishment, enlisting his support for the existing order. A bourgeois or aristocratic trick.[6]

Harry is agnostic, and a Labour Party man: his dad worked his guts out for the rights of the working man (to be accurate, for the rights of the members of his craft union); and no Tory – and no socialist intellectual, either – is going to rob him of them. Church, anyway, isn't for the likes of him, not his class. Otherwise, he's pretty well like Martin. As he gets older, and the conveyor belt looks to be accelerating, whatever the clock says, he's going to get badly depressed; and that'll slow him down worse. He'll join the ranks of faded shrivelled suppers of halves of mild, prematurely old. He'll not even feel the need to curse when the vicar calls. 'Jesus? The wife goes to the mothers' meeting. Here's ten bob for the box. Glad you called.'

Dick is happily employed and successfully married (the latter for the moment, anyway). He has arranged his life admirably, just as he planned it out in his teens. He is a gifted and safe stockbroker, with an attractive and wealthy wife. He enjoys watching other men envy him for her, and enjoys knowing that she is much too frigid sexually and much too independent intellectually for there to be much risk of his being cuckolded. They suit each other well. *His* tastes are far too odd to find scope among their circle of friends and acquaintances. When the black depression gets him, he goes away to one of a short list of

26

custom-equipped brothels, drinks, gets beaten, weeps for pardon, and is forgiven by a girl wearing a purple stole. He may become an alcoholic, but his wife knows of lots of expensive clinics. 'The suffering Christ, Bishop? I feel with him. . . .' His wife smiles, and he winks. 'But crucifixion? no, I confess I've never understood that.' 'Contemplate his sufferings, then', says the bishop, 'and maybe the symbol of the crucified will more deeply attract you.'

Tom, Dick, Harry, Martin, Nesta might all have had a sudden conversion in their teens; but now it is not very likely. They might be persuaded, even deeply persuaded. But that is not very likely either.

Austen is much more openly religious than all these. He sits every Sunday at the back of a church where the Mass is sung with beauty and precision in a haze of incense and plainsong, and the world is lost, with all its noise and uncertainty: though he prefers not to make his communion, because the movement and other people disturb him. He reads a lot; but sometimes the most terrible thoughts of lust and sadism drift into his mind, and he must make his confession, and then he thankfully receives the Body of Christ at an early Mass when there are not many people about. He lives with his sick mother and has a special devotion to the Mother of God. He is afraid that he is a homosexual. He does not mind other people's certainty that he is, but would like to disprove it to himself by marrying. He has been engaged twice, to nice motherly girls, but found he just had to break it off. The prospect of tying himself down, of close physical contact, almost literally unmanned him.

For him, Jesus is an ascetic, a man of prayer and strict discipline, a man apart, engaged in an unceasing inner dialogue with his Father. He is completely unaffected by the world. Jesus is a man who has been absorbed by God, so that physical impulses and emotions have no effect. God became man, to show us, and give us the way to overcome all earthly limitations, so our souls could be pure and united with God, and we would be lost in him, in the ocean of his love. Austen knows that this way of thinking about Jesus goes back into Christian history (to Christians in Alexandria), and that it too has been accepted as a right way of thinking since that same meeting at Chalcedon, A.D. 451. Further developments have reinforced this position. He believes (though it is difficult to express it without using the ancient terms, which Austen does not understand, though their lack of contact with today's world does strongly attract him) that the only reality in Jesus was (is) the reality of God. Any talk (in Nesta's terms) of Jesus *trying* to do what God wanted is nonsense. Jesus was God, God was the man Jesus, from conception through death and resurrection and into heaven; so that now there is nothing of the individual self of a man, Jesus. And this is wonderful. God became man, so that we could become divine, absorbed in God, lost in pure being, free from the world and the self that can oppress and distract. We can share, through prayer, sacraments, contemplation, in Jesus' complete self-emptying, self-destruction in sacrifice to the Father.[7]

Gupta equally finds the world around illusory, and whatever is really real must for him lie beyond things and beyond being an individual person. But for him, a claim to be the one true pointer to the really real is about the only claim that can have no truth. For the rest, everything there is can, more or less successfully, point through the illusion to reality beyond. Jesus, stripped of any claim to uniqueness, may do this. So may Hitler.

Jacqueline is hooked on Zen, coitus, and lysergic acid.

She is very gentle, and does not even hate violence violently. Jesus was gentle, but he did not have the courage to take the full way out of existing in the pain of being alive.[8]

Rudi and John are the next two jurors to be examined, before we can proceed to ourselves and to the Prisoner.

John is quite unlike Austen. Austen comes to life when he can retire into himself. John knows that he is in a great vacuum of loneliness. He knows that he can sometimes dispel this by bursts of activity, by attracting attention to himself. But there is a terror in this that is even worse. At the height of a madly gay party, he can realize that he is completely isolated, even from the girl he is entwined with. There is nothing and no one here that can give him a sense of being real, and he has no resources within himself. The closest he has come to finding relief has been in political action, in angry protest marches. There the activity continues, the cause is real. By any standards, there are real problems involved, Vietnam, race, the Bomb, hunger, unemployment. He is pleased to find Christians like Rudi on the long marches, but he cannot share their faith. There is nothing in his experience that justifies the degree of trust that seems to be expected. If the person is real that he is asked to believe in, then that person is responsible for John's loneliness and insecurity. And too many Christians seem content with this world that creates in John only an aching void, and will not join in the fight to force it into providing structures of love and meaningful reality.

Rudi was converted when he was in his teens, he made his decision, and surrendered himself to the Lord Jesus. So long as he does not assert his will against his Lord's will, all will be well, all will be very well. There are still moments of agonizing doubt about whether he is really accepted; but he reads and prays and sings the hymns of his childhood and makes himself very small, and he knows that he is back in the security of the one who loves him. Nothing that Rudi can do can win that love, and he knows that he cannot try and need not try. All that he must do is relax into the hands of the love that all the while enfolded him. It is only his struggling that prevents him from feeling and enjoying the ever-present care and self-giving of the Other who is completely his.

Austen's ('Alexandrian') terms for Jesus and God are the ones that Rudi can best use. Nesta's picture of Jesus the perfect man who is bound tight to God by his goodness and obedience to God's known will leaves Rudi (quite literally) cold. That would lack all security, all reality. In Jesus, God must have given himself completely and entirely to us, and to Rudi. An incarnation that depends on any worth in a man is useless; an incarnation in which there is even a logical possibility of God withdrawing just does not match the completeness of God's self-giving even to as worthless a creature as Rudi knows he is. God humbled himself, made himself of no account, just as Rudi finds he must.

Austen's God is One in three persons. The mystery attracts him, the depth of thought that must go into the doctrine. But for most intents and purposes, Austen's God is the same solitary being as Nesta's. Austen is most real alone; so is his God; and Austen contemplates God in Godlike quiet and solitude. For Rudi, obviously, this is impossible, it would be Hell. God is a company, a family in which two do not exclude a third, in which the three enfold a bustling living multitude. You might even doubt the love you sense, on your own: you doubt yourself so deeply that you doubt even your own sensations. But here you are part and parcel with others who from their security bolster yours. So doubt is dispelled. Or almost. Surely they could not all be pretending?

Rudi's faith does not prevent him from joining John in political activity. He finds that too long a time in the company of evangelical Christian friends allows doubts to re-form. He begins to suspect that the bright confidence is a partly hysterical mask for uncertainty, that everyone is trying to stand on everyone else's faith (not offering their faith for everyone else to rest on), and then it may all be illusion. So he turns to let his Lord meet him in ordinary everyday things, and worldly causes, and protesting enthusiasm. Finding a real power of goodness at work, his faith is refreshed. From there he can look forward to and really appreciate each home-coming, to be where he knows he really belongs, among those who love the Lord Jesus, and rest in his love.

I, the author of this book, am the eleventh member of this particular jury, and find myself in differing measure in all my fellow members. Or maybe I am all these and also a very different type from any of them, and just find it hard to sketch what predominates in myself. The distinctions between them have seemed useful to some psychologists, as working models, as subdivisions that prove useful in practice. There may be other charts that group them quite differently. There may be numerically or qualitatively important groups of types that I have neglected. These happen to seem to me to be ways of looking at God, at Jesus, at the world, that tie up significantly with dogmatic positions which Christians, agnostics, and atheists have adopted.

You, the reader, are my Siamese twin, at least till you shut the book, and manage to forget it. Even if you succeed in pulling me in exactly the opposite direction to that in which I hope to go, your steps are for the time being determined by mine, for it is against mine that you are moving. So, as you are for the moment my twin, I assume that you too find all these ways of seeing things in yourself. Now one predominates, now another. You are able to see something – even if different things – of the strengths and weaknesses, attractiveness and inadequacy of the various possible positions. If you are very predominantly of one type, I hope that you are able – or that being for the moment my twin makes you able – to see that other people live truly by other pictures and moods. (Do I need to say that if you are predominantly Nesta, Austen, Rudi, or any of the others, that does not make you, in the usual sense, 'unbalanced', or even particularly likely to be. It might just mean some psycho-analysts would find you easier to sort out.)

To see all this is not to abandon words like 'true' and 'false', 'right' and 'wrong', 'orthodox' and 'heretic', 'innocent' and 'guilty'. But you wait a while before using them, and you wait the longer the more critical the term is. And Nesta, Austen, Rudi, you, I and the rest will have each our own pattern of what is right and wrong thinking, for us, each our own heresy and orthodoxy. There is orthodox and heretical 'Nestorianism', and orthodox and heretical Christian tritheism *and* true and false Christian atheism; and so on.

And there are facts, welcome and unwelcome; and with a degree of self-knowledge you may come that bit closer to them.

You are the twelfth member of the jury, and its foreman. There is no judge, unless it is the Prisoner. And remember, the jury too is on trial. (But then, juries always are. That is why it has been the custom to choose jurymen with a strong stake in the established order. It helps keep them from convicting themselves and acquitting the accused).

# 3. The Man for Me[1]

He enjoyed being alive. He went to parties and drank – just as much as was good for him? I do not know. The people who got to dislike him said he ate and drank too much. But he accepted an invitation even from them.[2]

Parties mean people, and it was people he really wanted. You might say he used them. Any revolutionary seems to the outsider to be doing that. To the man and to his friends, he's sharing what really matters, and they'd not want less. Whether he ever relaxed with them, you can't say – except perhaps at parties. At times he seems austere, withdrawn – but there was something in him and his words that held some people. Perhaps he trapped them in a spell of words, dominated them by force of personality. Someone who sees himself as a servant can still gain control from below, as it were. But that, for sure, is not what they thought of him. There was no obvious plank in his eye to keep him from helping other people with their specks of sawdust – or planks. What he looked to be doing was simply accepting people as they were, just so long as they would let him. (Of course, they already had friends who accepted them as they were. Being accepted by this man with this programme was something different.) All sorts of unlikely people he made friends with. Looking back, anyway, they saw quislings and rebels, whores and crooks, ordinary decent working people, the sick who frighten you, cripples who make you feel sick, even one or two wealthy men.

Being his friend, saying Yes when he invited you, could cost some people a lot, cost them their wealth, cost them their respectability. You could not follow him round the countryside with the security of a big estate to fall back on. You could not join his rag-taggle mob and still feel easy with your law-abiding neighbours. And there'd always be a risk (I do not know how soon he or they realized this) that you'd end up on a gallows as a rebel. Nasty.[3]

He took you as you were, but you had to let some things go, just to be able to say Yes. Money and respectability were high on the list. But a lot of his friends didn't have either, so that bit wasn't too hard. Settled family life and your job, those would go if you travelled round with him. Other things had to go, too. Fussy anxiety, spite, wanting to get your own back, clinging on to the last few relics of what was yours. He'd needle you out of those. And out of too much ambition, refusing to accept and forgive the people round you the way you'd been forgiven and accepted. All this took longer, but you had to let it happen, you had to move. You had to swallow your pride, and take the new line, the new life, that he offered you.[4]

It was why he admired children. They'd take something good, if it was offered, even if it was new (or especially if it was new). There are hints (all these are only hints) that he enjoyed children the way someone can who accepts his own childhood.[5]

And yet he might ask you to break with all this – children, wife, the whole family that was wider still. You had to choose. You had to let him set you free from everything – or lots of things – in your past that held you. Set you free *for* the new things that would happen (it seems it could mean going back to your wife, family, job, but in a new way). He tried to free you from things lots would say were bad – and from things lots would say were good, too. Set you free to be a new man in a new world.[6]

It is this freedom of Jesus himself – a freedom he invited other people into, shared with them – that especially attracts at least the attention of some present-day observers at this distance. Jesus – Yeshua – was remarkably free within the Jewish way of life he was born to. For certain, there were areas of choice, freedoms of a sort, presented to others. You could be a Pharisee, or an Essene of some sort, you could be a Sadducee (or perhaps you could escape from being one, despite your birth), you could be a patriotic extremist; you could be an ordinary man. We still can only guess at the variety of positions that were possible. But in each grouping, the pressures to conform were immense, and to conform in precise and sometimes minute details. A Galilean fisherman might seem to a disapproving Pharisee to be leading a very free, positively libertine life. But the fisherman would find it appallingly hard to sit down to table with the nicest of non-Jews.

And if you did not wish to drift with the ordinary people around you, all the pressures were directed towards making you choose some smaller group's much stricter patterning of life. If you thought, if you took life seriously, the most readily available framework for thought suggested that

35

more and more possible situations should be classified, and the range of response and initiative should be narrowed to the precise, if often very complex, range of what could be foreseen.

The codes of behaviour that were built up often expressed a liberal and humane appreciation of life. They were by no means harsh and oppressive, certainly in intention. And a code that restricts my neighbour's power over me and prescribes his care for me can offer me and my community a freedom that might not otherwise be there. The complex rules of chess can give me more freedom than the simple rules of draughts.

But Jesus succeeded in breaking free from the best and most meaningful ways of life that were offered, breaking free into something more. He insisted on being more free for others than any available code allowed him to be. He did not even allow the codes, the patterns of behaviour, themselves to pattern his critical reaction to them. He would not allow their all-or-nothing claims to prevent him from sifting and judging them, and seizing on some of the insights and impulses that he saw lying at the heart of them. The restricted freedom that the codes gave me for (and from) my neighbour, Jesus set free from their self-imposed limits. My freedom for my neighbour was to have no limits, his freedom from me was to be limited only by his freedom for me. Life was not a game with rules for winning; if it was a game at all, it was one to be lost, by playing it harder than rules could ever envisage.

That is all rather abstract. But you see Jesus' freedom in his openness to people. He is open to the strong. He is open to the legal expert who finds the same heart in the code as Jesus found in it. 'Love God entirely. Love every man as you want to be loved.' He is open to John the Baptist, a man with a very different vision from his own, but a man who is trying to shake the nation out of its self-satisfaction; and Jesus includes himself among the disturbed and accepts baptism. He is open to the rich young man, if he will be accepted for himself, and give away his wealth. He is open, in his stories, to the foreigner who is simply good; to the kindly and generous who are themselves open to the weak and outcast. Jesus can admire the quick wit of the swindler who acts promptly – and still illegally – to get himself out of a tight spot, the trader and the broker with a keen eye for a quick profit.[7]

Jesus is shown meeting opponents on their own ground, where they are strong, challenging them to a deeper commitment to a trust he still feels in some sense they do share with him. When he sits down and thinks, is there anything that a Jew may withhold from his God? and what does that mean to his hearers in terms of practical politics – Caesar, and all that? Can a Jew really believe that his God will ever leave go of him – surely neither death nor wife can break his grip? He defends his acceptance, as friends and followers, of outcasts who let themselves be accepted. Isn't that the way a father would want to treat a son who was lost to him, come what may? Even a sheep farmer wouldn't do less for a stray animal.[8]

And he goes to Jerusalem, to put himself completely in the hands of the strong men who can brush him aside with a soon forgotten flick of a hand. Jesus is open to the strong at the points of their strength, and meets them there. And suffers.[9]

Jesus is open to the weak – to draw them out of their weakness. To the adulteress, 'Go, I don't condemn you; but do not do it again!' (Of course he may have said more, you cannot argue from the shortness of the stories. But there is no record of Jesus moralizing in these situations, 'Go home, and be very sorry, plead with God for forgiveness, make amends.') To the woman who came in to the dinner party (in Luke's story), 'Your sins are forgiven.'[10]

'Your faith has made you well, whole, saved you.' It sounds rather like a formula, a tag to pop into the story (wherever the story came from). But if you take it as a formula of Jesus' own, he looks hard to find a point of strength in the person who feels only weakness. (He could have said, 'Grovel, and God – or I – will pity you'; and kept them weak and inescapably humble. He could have said, 'Forget it' – and they could not, and would have stayed in their welter of guilt. 'Do something that will take your mind off it' – and that just rubs in the fact that you can't, you know it, you've tried.) Instead, 'you have already reached out', says Jesus, 'for the new life I offer you.' You have done it – you who thought you could do nothing. (Of course it is a pure gift, and you did not earn it. He does not have to say that. He says, 'It is a gift that you have already accepted.') Jesus is open to the weak, to make them strong.[11]

'It isn't those who are well that need a doctor, but those who are sick. I didn't come to call the good, but the wicked.' Is that a joke? Is anyone well? Jesus berates the good for the limiting of their goodness, the righteous for their self-righteousness. The Pharisee in the Temple is a lot further from his God than the tax collector who asks God to take him as he really is. But the half-good are good, the self-righteous are in part really right. Jesus does not try to destroy or hamstring with guilt the goodness and strength that is there; but to point it to where it should go. And so the anger when no move is made. Of those who are given a lot, a lot is asked. Jesus' first job is not to make the strong feel like the weak, to make them feel that they need God and Jesus. He is open to the strong, and will deal with them when they present themselves. His first job is to fetch the guilty out of their guilt, the outcasts out of their rejection, the poor out of their hopelessness, the sick out of their feebleness; so they can look the past in the face, and live. So he is open to the penitent whore, the quisling tax collector, the beggar, the outcast leper, the neurotic sick, the paranoid madman.[12]

His care for the sick attracts; the picture of the miracle-worker is now more likely to repel. The care which the modern Roman Catholic Church finds necessary in investigating claims for miracles shows how easy it is for accounts of them to be invented, in all sincerity, 'even' today. For an extraordinary claim, a modern man tends to need extraordinarily good evidence. Even if the gospels are good enough to trust for ordinary sounding stories, for ones like these you need almost – or quite – impossibly good evidence. That does not prove they did not happen, and happen much as suggested. It means that there is no account available capable of persuading me, and others.

(Perhaps this is a little too sweeping. A percentage of seemingly incurable cases do get better – with no common factor, chemical or 'religious', at present discernible. And some diseases have a more or less largely psychosomatic origin, or are accompanied by symptoms caused or exaggerated this way. To be accepted by a man as free and as open as this Jesus could well have dealt with symptoms or even with underlying causes. Maybe he did heal some. But certainly sickness and health mattered to him.)

There is no telling how good his own health was (why is he always pictured so sound in wind and limb?). But for sure, at the end, he himself accepted pain and death and loss of all the good he had enjoyed. For some reason, it was worth risking. It was all so good that it was worth risking it all. He had lived for the weak and the not so weak

39

to let them be strong; and now he had to lay himself open to the goodness and the sense and the wickedness of the strong at the point of their strength, in the city of Jerusalem.

And this was a man who himself enjoyed being alive, so it seemed, and could savour a wide range of the life that lay around him. This is no less real for its especial appeal to last century's romantic lovers of 'nature' and this century's bird fanciers and dog-lovers. Men at work, and the frequent failure and odd success that follows haphazard sowing. Fishing, house building, finance and trade. Pestering neighbours and nagging old women. House-keeping, cookery, parents and children. Children at play, children and parents. Harvest of corn, grapes, olives, figs. The manners of high officials, the prattle of gossips. Stylized observation of the weather, commonplace humour at the expense of camels and other creatures proud and ungainly, and the inevitability of carrion birds. Weddings, funerals, childbirth; war and desolation and feasting and forgetting. And the royal red flowers and the sparrow.[13]

All these mattered, they were worth noting and articulating, and impressing on the memories of those around. These were all part of a man's world – this man's world – and so they could tell him about himself and his friends and enemies, could point beyond themselves to the men for whom they were there. They could point to men in their essence, person with person, the enriching of love. They were there for men, and to point to men and love, because men and love mattered so much, and so much more than all these. And more than these, and more than men, but not apart from men (unless men insisted, and not finally even then) is God.[14]

Men matter so much to Jesus, and God is so close to men, that you can see Jesus' openness to men and their world (which is above all, Jesus' own world) without for a long while mentioning God more than in passing. But Jesus without God is a distortion, a parody. Whatever I make of God, Jesus 'knew' that what mattered was what God made of him. Jesus is open to God, free for God.[15]

God for you and me is an unrealized ideal, a pattern of commitment, a projection of fears and fancies, a wish for a real parent, a retreat to infancy—or maybe something, someone, like Jesus' God. Father? Dad(dy)? my Old Man? love and respect – respect for love, not the perverted pleasure of respectful cringing. God, and deep excitement. God close, God about to rule, in love and fire. There's a feasting to look forward to!

Jesus is open to men and his world; but he is not an open vacuum, because his openness is firstly openness to his God. Free for men and his world, but not aimless, because God is his goal to which he freely runs, and it is God who first moved him.

There are different freedoms, and gain one, you lose another. This is his freedom, in which he lives, and which makes him open and able to invite and share. This is the rule of God – Jesus' God – the kingdom of this God: the gift of this freedom for others, the freedom to serve (and to serve without corrupting).

Jesus is the herald of this kingdom. He is that and more, he is the vice-regent and vice-gerent of this rule of this God. Men might want a kingdom of their God in which their warrior hate could rule, in which their censorious conscience might rule and condemn and be gracious to the frightened and cringing. A kingdom where their lust, greed, cruelty, vengefulness, guilt, pride, could rule and be made respectable and admirable because they would know it was really God's, not theirs at all (they are kind and generous), and it would have infinite power and wisdom behind it, and that would make it right – somehow. But

41

Jesus said, 'That is not the sort of power and rule that you are to admire and live by.' (Could Jesus still have allowed them to project all this on God, and make God Judge, Tormentor, Destroyer? Could he? Did he? If he did, then I have to falsify the record of Jesus the theologian in favour of the truth of Jesus the man. But I think the evidence is good enough that he was consistent here too.) 'I am the herald,' he said, 'the vice-gerent of the rule of this God, and I am this sort of man.' A man greatly free, free enough to serve, and share freedom (not devour it in parasitic servility) by serving. On Jesus – in Jesus – is focused the rule of this God.[16]

Jesus is accepted by his God. This he knows. He does not know that he is good. He certainly does not 'know that he is God'. He knows that he is accepted by God, ruled by God, fired by God. By this God. Father and son. In the power of this acceptance, he dares to act for God. Because he is accepted, he is free to accept others, forgive, renew. His God may lure him into wild dreams of harvest and home-coming and feasting for the poor and the feckless. His God may make him stand for the nation against the nation. He is so wholly for God that later they will say he tried to act instead of God. But he is accepted by his God who chooses to come to rule this way, by accepting, forgiving, setting free.[17]

There are different kinds of freedom. This is the freedom of knowing that – against all appearance, maybe – you are already at home. However hard you have to fight to enjoy what is yours, it is yours. However tempting it may be to try to lose what you have been given, you cannot earn it, you may not try to earn it, it has been already granted. Your God is yours, and your neighbour is yours and the world is yours.[18]

You do not earn this life: but you are and will be

extravagantly rewarded. You do not find your satisfaction in yourself (you can try to lose it that way). You do not find your satisfaction in possessions – spiritual, personal, intellectual, material – with which you could arm yourself against God, men, the world, life. A stronger than you would come – if you were lucky – and despoil you of them. God is given to you – by God: you are his. The world is given to you to inherit. Your neighbour is given to you – to be loved by, and to love. This is appallingly a-moral, immoral, libertine. And this is the freedom that Jesus enjoyed, and the freedom into which he invited the weak and the strong.[19]

Because he is accepted by his God, and free in this way, Jesus can face the demands of the freedom God gives, and can make them known. Anyone can listen. Those who have accepted his God's acceptance of them, and have allowed Jesus to share with them his freedom, can hear. They may allow this God to love them, they may let their neighbour love them, they may live this freedom in the world around.

Any man may be the man who graciously (ungraciously, unconsciously) allows me to care for him. He is this man who has met me. Because I am free to be loved by him, I am free at least to hope that he will accept my gift, and accept even my caring and my loving.

If I share Jesus' freedom, I may even dare to let a man hate me, insult me, torture me. To let him do these things could be my cruellest act of spite and revenge. But sharing Jesus' freedom, I may even make this vicious masochism an act of love. I can stand for a man's dear and hated parents and siblings, for the repression of his lust, for the rending, crushing violence of his conscience and guilt – and not add to his guilt and self-contempt and fury, but be the point where he finds himself and his freedom. I can be the point where a man loosens his lingering grasp on the guilt that he holds most precious, the possession that is most inalienably his.[20]

If a man can do that for me, if I can do that for a man, then there is nothing that I cannot do. I can give him my coat, my food, my money. I can see a man's life grow as he forgets his hunger and cold and loneliness and fear, and my own life grows because it is bounded by one less weight on my shoulders, and my world is larger.

If I am poor, then my life is cramped into a vision of a fire and a loaf and a cup; if I am rich, I have a larger cell, but my horizon is bounded by even firmer limits. Sharing Jesus' freedom I can give and receive, it does not matter which, either way my world will grow.

I can risk the uncertainty of owning very little; and forgo the anxious security of owning more and more, and acquiring more and more to secure what I already have; even forgo the greater ascetic security of owning nothing at all. I can accept the insecurity of depending on other people. (Is all this possible in a technologically complex modern society? Men say it was well enough in peasant days. But today I cannot escape from depending on other people; in a simple farm economy, I might.) I may depend for much more than food. I can depend on others for every word that comes from the mouth of this God. I may well be his lips to them. The vice-gerent of God's vice-regent.[21]

Once for a lifetime, I may give myself entirely, a man to this woman, woman to this man, share our brute and tender pleasure, risk its ecstasy and loss, be real. I can risk a self-giving so final and threatening and full of uncertain promise. He tells me his God would have it this way.

From the freedom of his acceptance by his God (and by his friends) Jesus dares to penetrate to the centre of my

44

being as a person, and demand that I be free there. If he can reach as far as my guilt, then for sure he can reach to my hate and possessive lust and my sworn hostility to truth. He can make an impossible demand on me, because he has already given me a share in an impossible freedom; and if he has not, I shall listen to his voice, and not hear him (but hear, instead, Kant or my Sunday School teacher or a second Moses or my demonic conscience).

This is the way the freedom goes which he offers. He will let me see the world as a place where Yahweh plays Dionysus and sends an open invitation to his party; and when I arrive, I shall find I am not a duty-guest but a son of the house among my brothers. I can scatter what I have prodigally, irresponsibly, quite selfishly, and find an absurdly rich return. I can lose everything, and find that I have more than I started with. I can even imperil my soul by sweating my guts out, and find that I still have only what I need of what this God gives: and it is still a gift given, though I tried to lose it by earning it. It is a world where anything can happen, at any time, and be good; so it is worth while being awake. (But it is better to read it in the words and stories and pictures they say he used. I refer you to the notes and so to the Gospels.)[22]

He acted as God's vice-regent. Take away every hint of this, and you are left with a blank that only he can fill, or we must arbitrarily ignore. Accept that he did, as a working hypothesis, and you still have to work out, how, and in which of the words and stories and pictures that are put on his lips. He had a rich palette from which to choose, a large range of models from which he could draw: the Jewish scriptures, the varied tradition from then till his own day, the world around. But it was not an unlimited palette, and his friends who embroidered with and on his words had much the same materials, and more, to use. Sorting what he said then from what they said later is difficult. The choice on which the foregoing is based is defended – lightly – in the notes. It is still important to debate whether – and then, in what sense – he may not only have acted as God's vice-regent, but have in conscious reflection called himself that. For all the complexity and tentativeness of the critical sorting out, we still need to ask, 'Did he call himself "the Messiah" – or anything of the sort? Or did he just act for God without putting a title to his role?'[23]

The claims Jesus makes for himself in the fourth gospel (called John's) are those that 'John' places on his lips. They are related to things Jesus may have said, and help to illustrate them. They articulate a penetrating commitment to Jesus, and as such I draw on them gratefully. They tell us nothing that Jesus himself said; nothing, that is, that can be accepted apart from, still less in contradiction to, the first three gospels. It is on the first three that we concentrate, straining to hear the whisper that may shatter us.

That Jesus called himself 'Son', and meant the eternal companion of the eternal Father and Creator, visitor to Palestine in human disguise, has been believed, but lacks any good evidence. Nor did he let himself be called 'Lord', as a masquerading deity. (Such a Son belongs to a different father, such a Lord to some other domain. Jesus was free, but his freedom was far from that of an all-absorbing vacuum. At least, I have suggested that his freedom lay in a liberating, unservile service; not in a sovereignty that is captive to those to whose servility it panders. This is by way of reminder; the arguments are set out above.)

Hardly less improbable is the view that he let himself be called God's Anointed, the Messiah, the Christ. The first three gospels (the 'synoptics') give him the title sparingly, and rarely without allowing him to protest: 'Those are your words, not mine'. The Führer, El Cid, M, the Arthurian King, David *redivivus* bloody-handed. (Of course, Jesus, too, did end up with bloodstained hands.) He could have accepted the title and turned it inside out. But he did not come to rule by force, not even by the force of a torrent of brain-washing words (which is the gentlest image the title would have conveyed).

He came, he lived, loved, died, as a man. Perhaps he did call himself the Man, Everyman, the representative suffering man. He dared to live as *the* free man, *the* Jew, the man in whom the world and Israel could find God's freedom, the man against whom all other freedom could be measured. So perhaps he did use the enigmatic humbling-proud title, the Son of Man. (Of all the titles that look like titles, there is best evidence for this, though it is not very good, and it is at least as much disputed as the others.) And anyway, he was a man who was the pattern of what his God meant men to be, the pattern he had always intended.

He was a prophet, a man who gave away costly visions, and pointed to his God who was his father. A prophet who witnessed to the truth of his God was bound to suffer in Israel. A less moral people might have ignored him. But it is not nice to have someone commit Jesus' acts of love in public.

If a witness to God's truth suffered for God's truth, so the belief went, that would set God's people free for God's truth, purge them, cleanse them. If a man were completely open and free to his God, completely free and open to men around, with this openness and this freedom to the point of death, then his freedom and openness could be shared. Jesus carried his unguarded liberty to the cross. Maybe he believed this was how his God meant him

47

finally to share it. Redemption, manumission, setting free.[24]

It does not have to work. The vision for which a man dies must often die with him. There is no sociological law to guarantee a dying gift of life. The death for God and men is itself a part of the vision.

And twenty years later, Paul said, 'In Christ you are set right with God, and free for God and free for each other.' The vision *was* shared; the price was paid, and our freedom was bought. This freedom – well, more or less closely related freedoms – can still be had. Have you not found it so?[25]

The vision was shattered, and lived in parts, re-made, spoiled, destroyed, enhanced. And the man? He had been the bearer of the vision, the vice-regent of the rule of God. They said he lived, as a man to be touched. Transformed, to be sure. But the tomb was empty. They were sure of the miracle. There is no second miracle to persuade me of it. There is no evidence possible good enough for me to call this a fact, a deed that was done, however generous I may be with the award of 'fact' to other hints and possibilities. That the vision does not end with the death of the seer – even for the seer himself – I may believe. I can choose to say, 'He is risen.' I cannot choose (though you may), I am not free to, to say it the way Peter and Paul did (much though I may regret this. Still less am I free to make Paul and Peter say it my way).

He died. He really died. He trusted his God, he trusted the Father who accepted him. In the power of this acceptance he was free for the world around, and for the weak and the strong in Jerusalem; and so he was free to lose them, for them. For his freedom was the gift of his God, and this was his God's way of opening still wider the invitation to be accepted, and accept, to be loved and to love. He put even his trust in his God at hazard; and they say he lost even that, for us.

He left words and pictures and stories and friends and a party to celebrate. And whether you choose to say he is alive, or whether you choose to say, 'Of course he is dead', you may still share his freedom, among his words and pictures and stories and the friends at the party. But that is what the rest of the book is about.

The man for me. As it happens, I am caught. Childhood, family, friends, education, the psychology of me, its needs and projections and wish fulfilments, social pressures, my job as a clergyman: all these, and pictures of him, often quite like the one above have me caught. So I have to refer back, and look again. Not to a living image, not even to a shadow now behind me. Others I live among, have met, read of, are much livelier. But for freedom and judgement and fire and life and caring, I have to look back just here, to this Jesus, to see what I may this time see. (And trust him for his God who will not have let him down; nor me.)

Obviously, he is not every man's Everyman. He belongs firmly (and that means for some, exclusively) to first-century Galilean Judaism. His beliefs about the structure of total reality were in mythological terms; many of his beliefs include factual claims which are either untrue or nonsense.

He believed that the rule of God was going to happen, it was going to be obvious, accepted, on a large and inescapable scale, very soon. At the latest it would be not long after his death: as God's gift, God's act, with men responding, for or against. It is impossible to rid what he is said to have said of this prediction, without violent distortion of the whole. It was, is, part of the vision, to see it so clearly and gladly that it must soon shape all there is. For sure, there are other ways of expressing urgency in all this, but this was his way, and he was wrong. And his mistake repels honest men. How can his vision of God's intervention and reshaping of the universe for love and freedom be mine, how can any of the demands that Jesus made in the context of his freedom and acceptance be demands to us when he was so deeply wrong? We cannot pretend to see the world suddenly renewed, it just is not a live option. Maybe a Marxist could see it; we, in the liberal, evolutionary West, just cannot, except stagily, artificially: and then where is the promised freedom? And the demons, and the view of history, and the picture of the physical universe. All these can cut him off from us.

Even for his own time, he had little constructive to say about the political, economic, and social matters that concern me. 'Give back to God what belongs to him' may be good theology, or individual ethics; it says nothing about the responsible use of power by Caesar then, and so nothing from which we may extrapolate to our own political situation. The repetition of a primitive psychophysiological tag from Genesis tells us nothing about monogamy or polygamy, about the abuse of sexuality in marriage, about freedom against a background of promiscuity. He tells us nothing about population control. How do we defend our neighbours from our friends? If we really take no thought for tomorrow – or even, none for next year – we will have no coat to give to him who asks, and we, being evil, will have only stones for our children (and our neighbours' children). The care he demanded for the sick and poor and hungry and imprisoned comes through organized capitalism or through state planning or through systematic voluntary activities: but he gave no obvious, no explicit impetus to find them. For sure, his vision may have helped. It may – let's be kind – have helped more than hindered. But now it is not needed.

And an adult twentieth-century man may find no place for the sort of hero-worship that focuses on Jesus. If he does, he may prefer a pan-andron, a gallery of heroes; or some other man, Socrates, Bertrand Russell. But he may find no need to collect his ideals and commitments into any personified form, real or imaginary.

That this may be so for him, and for many like him, I have to accept. It is not so for me. For me, Jesus (in one or other of the ways I see him) is the man, the man for me.

# 4. The God for Me: the Logic of Love[1]

WE HAVE seen that to raise the question of Jesus is likely to raise the question of God; and certainly questions of my self, and of men and the world around me. I have confessed that I am myself deeply involved.

I want to respond positively, and fully, to this Jesus that I have tried to sketch; and that involves me in a response to his God. He is presented to me – or different impressions of him are presented to me – by the various Christian communities, present and past. It is among them that I find his memory preserved in a living response. And most of them say, This Jesus *is* God.

What sense, if any, can I make of that? I have said that I am persuaded by contemporary scholars (and a certain amount of personal research) that it is very unlikely that Jesus called himself 'Christ', let alone 'Son of God'; and as nearly certain as may be that he did not even entertain the suspicion that he might somehow 'be' God. How, then, can current 'orthodox' Christian belief be right? In its own terms, how could Jesus 'be' God, without knowing it? You could hardly be said to 'be' even a fictional character without your own knowledge.

Further, philosophers of the 'linguistic analysis' school (and my own researches in this field) have persuaded me that much traditional language about Jesus and God and Jesus' humanness – 'substance', 'nature', *persona* – produces barely concealed contradictions. In fact, many of the terms used in theology – 'infinite', 'ineffable', the word 'God' itself – often appear in sentences so sense less that it is hard to know even how to agree or disagree with them. Yet I still want to respond to this Jesus and to his God, presented to me by these varied communities; though it is largely in this sort of language that they are offered.[2]

## (i) 'God'

First the noun–name–title 'God'. 'Money is his God' means that the lust for wealth patterns this or that man's life. He is committed to it. This is the drive he obeys. And this illustrates at least a part of common usage of the word. It is certainly a large part of what Old Testament writers meant by 'God', or so the scholars suggest. Of course, 'God' meant necessarily a real and powerful and active being; but if you did not understand him as a demand on you that you had to obey, then you had very largely misunderstood him. 'I am Yahweh your God, you shall . . .' God is he who demands, elicits, and one way or another enables your obedience to himself. He is more, but he is pre-eminently this.

I find it meaningful to start with this (part of the)

53

meaning of 'God', if only to move on from there if I can. And quite a few modern philosophers and theologians agree in finding the most nearly intelligible area of religious language just here. It is a way of expressing what 'I' intend to do, the pattern of behaviour 'I' intend to follow. It provides a 'model' for the activity of living. (We shall look a bit more at this sort of suggestion in the next chapter.)

In the New Testament, the pattern of obedience, the insistent invitation to obedience, the empowering of obedience spring from, centre upon, Jesus. 'Let your attitude to one another arise out of your life in Christ, who himself accepted the life of a slave, and was obedient right up to death.' This is what it means – this is a very large part of what it means – for Jesus to be 'Lord'. 'Jesus is Lord' *means*, above all, that every created being will bow at his name, bow to his will.[3]

Of course, as we have already seen, this is a new sort of obedience. It is not the obedience of a slave who cringes, of the servant who must earn his way. It is obedience in terms of love, demanded by a Lord who is love, a Lord who is himself a servant. But obedience it is. Jesus is *Lord*, and the Christian is his slave: a slave captivated and liberated in one by love.

Jesus is the demand, the pattern, and the compelling invitation to obedience. At least in this sense (if in no other) for the Christian, Jesus is 'God'. No one else demands and shapes the Christian's obedience (no one else, that is, is meant to do this). Jesus allows no other master to compete for our allegiance. 'Follow me!' Buddha, and Allah, and Krishna, and the Idea of the Good, and Yahweh himself; my state, my class, my church, my family, my self can command only when Jesus speaks through them, or at least does not contradict them. Even

54

an uncertain whisper from him must carry above the shouts of all who would gainsay him.

The demand for obedience is no less insistent for being, for most of us, unclear. We have (I have) no infallible Book, Casuistry, Conscience or Reason for guide. And yet, within this lawless uncertainty, as a Christian I am called to obey Jesus as God.

I have insisted that this is not all that 'Jesus is Lord', 'My Lord and my God', meant to the writers whose books make up our New Testament literature. But it is only this element that can at all easily be shown to make sense to many of my contemporaries, and to me. 'Your God', 'my God', is what we obey. And if this allegiance, submission, commitment, love, are lacking, there is small point in talking of 'God' at all; little point in saying 'Lord, Lord', or 'Good Master'. If Jesus does not elicit obedience from his self-styled adherents, then he has failed the most basic test, the only at all widely recognized test of deity. He may even 'be there', but he is *roi fainéant*, irrelevant.

This is a serious matter. Christian Churches, going their own sour ways, look to be saying, loud and clear, 'There is no God.' Churches and individuals, you and I, spending vast sums on the splendour and comfort of our worship, on the comfort and variety of our own lives, in the face of a starving world, are saying to that world, 'No, you have made a mistake. Jesus of Nazareth is not our God.' Christian disobedience, wilfulness, selfishness are clear demonstration to most that Jesus is not God, or Lord, or really worth considering. It is so clear that it is almost impossible to *talk* usefully of him at all to most of our western contemporaries. He (or some other 'God') may 'be there'; but it is quite impossible to speak meaningfully of either.

55

Among people who do want to live committed to Jesus, it is still just possible to talk of 'God', of Jesus and 'God'. There are Christians – little old ladies, gentle and strong religious, near-inarticulate craftsmen, mothers with children, men of business, even some clerics – whose obedient love does face the rest of us with the Lordship of Jesus, the Godhead of Christ. The shape and style of their lives and love judge us, enable us, tell us: 'Here Jesus is God.' At least at these points, and among consenting members, it does still make sense to talk this way.

## (ii) Dead or alive?

It might seem that this is as far as someone with my presuppositions can go. And certainly, if talk of 'God', and of Jesus as 'God', is not justified at this level, there is not much to be gained in trying to go beyond this. We shall hardly persuade others that we have any further 'knowledge of God' to share, if what we have said so far has no noticeable echo in life. Silence would be more fitting.

Because of this difficulty of talking meaningfully of 'God' in the contemporary world, quite a few prominent Christian thinkers have concluded that 'God is dead'. He is treated as dead by so many who claim him, that the question of God has ceased to be a live issue. People are not committed to him; and they do not need him.

It was people's *need* of God – as physician, psychiatrist, fertilizer, weather expert, international diplomatist, cosmic explanation, lifeboat, welfare agency – that mainly kept the question of God in wide circulation. But now he is not needed as prop and support. It then becomes apparent that he has been and is little heeded as commanding and captivating and liberating Love. And so he seems as good (or bad) as dead.

But suppose (if only for argument's sake) that talk of Jesus as 'God', in terms of the 'pattern of obedience', *is* meaningful; can we say more? Traditional usage talks of 'God' who is objectively 'other', the Subject who confronts me as a real 'Thou' to my 'I'; a being who acts.

If I am to make my own something of the very varied New Testament response to Jesus as a commanding pattern of life, then I must in fact make some sense of the New Testament writers' insistence that the love Jesus demands is a love that is grateful to God who empowers it: 'Herein is love, not that we loved God, but that he loved us.' When this love, in which Christ is Lord, catches sight of its own achievements, it says, 'I, yet not I, but the grace of God which was with me.' When it looks forward to its own sure failure to break out of selfishness, it must be able to say, 'Who will set me free from the body of this death? I thank God through Jesus Christ our Lord.' Certainly for most New Testament writers, a Christian's love and caring and freedom are not the result of a lone struggle to imitate Jesus. They are something empowered by God, through Jesus who is alive. And this colours deeply and pervasively the sort of love and freedom and caring that are lived.[4]

It may mean, of course, that precisely this sort of New Testament ethic is closed to us; it just is not possible with any integrity to trust Jesus as the gracious act of a living God. We cannot, we may feel, live out our lives as men accepted by God through Jesus, for there is no meaning for us in talk of a God whose acceptance, justification, we could trust. It may be that the nearest we can approach to the New Testament and traditional Christian life, is to be empowered by the attractiveness of Jesus and the followers of Jesus. 'Not I, but the charm of the man who once charmed some fellow Jews; and charmed them still more powerfully after his death, when they thought back to him.'[5]

In a sense the question, How close is this to the sort of response that the New Testament writers hoped to make? is a straightforward question of observable behaviour. It is not a matter of verbal equivalence so much as one of active reproduction. Will a man committed to Jesus in these terms reproduce the expected results, 'the harvest of the Spirit'? Will he, in some real way, 'share Jesus' freedom'? If he does, then the difference is largely verbal, and of no great importance.

I do not want to prejudge the issue. If I myself at times trust in a powerful, gracious, enabling God, it would hardly be consistent to deny or even begrudge him the freedom to save for love how and where he wills. But it still seems to me that a way of life based on the attractiveness of Jesus is quite considerably different from a way of life based as much or more on a trust in the living power of the God of this Jesus, his present caring and love. The difference seems to me large enough (at least at the theoretical outset) for it to be worth persevering in my attempt to make as much my own as I may of this latter, more traditional response.

It is just the difference between my living my life in the trust that I am myself nice enough for the figure of Jesus, as I see him, to elicit a positive response from me; and living as one who trusts someone else so to cope with my self-concern that I may become loving (and attractable). If there is no God to work his works in me, then Jesus may be for me solely a judge who condemns me to a paralysing sense of my own inadequacy. There is then no receiving of freedom, only a clear despairing knowledge of the strength and restriction of my chains.

# (iii) Thoughtful wishing

Obviously, my crying desire for God, for God in moments of gratitude, in times of success and times of despair, does not show that there is anyone to answer my cry. All that it shows with any certainty is something of the sort of person that I am, or think I am. Yet I do want to trust such a God. I am attracted by the sort of ethic variously presented in the New Testament and in later Christian tradition. I want as much of it as I may for my own.

So I do trust, among the many inter-related shifting images that Christianity presents to me, one such transient image of the living God of Jesus Christ.

My trust may seem odd, but it is not unparalleled or necessarily pathological. It is very like the trust a man offers his wife, or she him, when they 'throw themselves away' on each other.[6]

We shall return to this point again in the next chapter. For the moment, I will only assert that it does make sense to me to say to my God: 'Though my childhood image of you appears now almost totally inadequate, and though words and images that once conveyed a sense of your reality now convey little or nothing, yet I trust you. What I can still imagine of you – though it can only seem imagination – demands that I trust you, though I can have no proof that you are real.'

Some object to Pascal's gamble. I am (and others are) quite prepared to take one form of it. *I am willing to gamble my life – or at least some parts of it – on the God that Christian tradition allows me to imagine being real and being love that will take us above any love we have known or dreamed of.* Of course, we may have lost before we started: there is no such prize to be won. But it will have been an exciting play, none the less.[7]

My trusting this God does not make me have to go back on any of the critical positions to which I have referred. I am still sure that any careful critical analysis of talk of this God must conclude that on a factual, verifiable or falsifiable level it is non-sense, and must classify it as 'myth' or, more bluntly, fiction. On any criteria that I dare to label 'objective' (even though that can only mean 'predominantly objective') talk of 'God' can appear only as a story. To some it is an attractive set of tales, to some entertaining, to some outgrown, to some dull, to some quite reprehensible. Some do find themselves trusting, committed.

If there really is God, if this word, which has no objective, testable descriptive content, none the less does have reference, then a trust like this is justified. If it does not seem worth while trusting God this far, if you are not free to leap before you can look, then certainly, for you there is no God worth trusting at all. If such a God as you thought you had is not worth this risk, he is worth nothing. At our best moments we do offer our God this unconditional trust. Love responding to the love we have glimpsed and heard tell of can do no less.

This God is obviously 'personal', and this talk about him has all the advantages of 'anthropomorphism' and 'myth'. There are other people for whom abstract talk about God as 'beyond personality', 'ultimate concern', 'the ground of being', makes good sense; some for whom these terms alone may make any sense at all. This is just another way of thinking; it is not natural to me; I am happy if others find it useful. It is not more 'true', or necessarily 'more adult'. A faith in a non-personal God may as well be a retreat to a pre-infantile, foetal stage of being, absorbed in the ground of being. It has its own sort of promise, and its own dangers. If it encourages a retreat from the risk of existing as personal, then it is bad. If it allows a genuine sense of enablement and creative freedom and openness to others, then it can do in other ways what I am trying to do here. For me, talk of God as 'a person' is essential to the pattern of enabled love by which I hope to live. This God is the God that Jesus addressed as 'abba'; the way a grown-up son talks to a parent who loves him, the parent he loves.[8]

## (iv) Godlike – or God

If, then, Jesus is to be my 'God' at least in the sense of the commanding pattern of my life, I must believe in the gracious God that he called 'Father'. Jesus is God as my pattern, only if I trust God himself to mould my life to be like Jesus' life.

Allowing this, what is the relation of Jesus to the God I find I must talk of, the God who enables my response, the God he called Father? Can I call Jesus himself 'God'?

Some Christians (Nesta, in our jury, for instance) find it sufficient to believe that Jesus just gives us the clearest picture we have – even the clearest we could have – of this God; and so in Jesus we are able to 'see' this God. Jesus is 'transparent' to God. Jesus, on this view, is related to his God as the most inspired, even the (only) perfectly obedient saint. Those who say this would often insist that they thereby maintain the traditional insistence on the uniqueness of Jesus' relation to his God. They say they are saying the most that can meaningfully be said, and it can be said only of him. Jesus is the highest instance of the general revealing and redeeming activity of God his Father. And they add that to try to find 'more' of God in Christ would be to make nonsense of traditional belief in God's omnipotence, omnipresence, omniscience; and probably to make nonsense of Jesus' humanity. This is all linked, as I have already mentioned, with what is technically known as the 'Antiochene' view of Christ. Jesus is not to be called 'God'.[9]

I want to suggest three reasons why I find this only very partially satisfactory; inadequate, in fact, to express the sort of commitment to Jesus that I wish to make.

Firstly, even on its own terms, is the Antiochene revealer-saint view of Christ sufficient? If God *is* revealed in Jesus, then God is humble, loving, willing to serve. If God is not like that, Jesus misleads us. But if God *is* humble, loving, willing to serve, how can he get someone else to reveal this for him? A proud man can have another reveal his pride for him; a humble man can only himself reveal his own humility. When a sovereign gets some other person to perform the royal Maundy foot-washing for him, he does not in that reveal humility. If Jesus is to reveal the humility of God, he must in some definite sense 'be' that God.

However, I cannot myself believe that it was the purpose of the God I trust in to reveal himself in Christ. (I have argued this at some length in another book.) He just does not seem to be revealed. Those of us who one way or another claim him can argue till the shift comes home (and we do) as to what this supposedly revealed God is like, and intends for us.[10]

Instead, with many New Testament writers, and Christians since, I believe that God's purpose in Christ was to save us, set us free, from ourselves; and change us, for ourselves, for others, for himself: until finally we reach the point where we *may* see him clearly. 'Revelation' is not his purpose until then, and he remains hidden. But God could not be loving us into loving one another and him in Jesus, if Jesus were not in some sense 'God'. Even if it makes sense to talk of 'revealing' another's love, you cannot actually yourself love at second hand. How could God *be* love, and ask someone quite other than himself to hang on a cross to express his love for him? How could God love through another's pain and loneliness? If Jesus is the saving of the world for love and so for God, if Jesus is the love of God for the world, then Jesus must 'be' 'God'.

What I want to say next is well put by Sidney Carter in his ballad (much quoted recently in this sort of context):

### Friday Morning

You can blame it onto Adam,
You can blame it onto Eve,
You can blame it on the apple,
But that I can't believe.
It was God who made the Devil
And the Woman and the Man,
And there wouldn't be an apple
If it wasn't in the Plan.
  It's God they ought to crucify
  Instead of you and me,
  I said to the carpenter
  A-hanging on the tree.

To be a committed Christian in this kind of world is only tolerable if I may believe that the carpenter was God allowing himself to be crucified. Jesus is God accepting crucifixion to atone for loving us so greatly that he created us, and created us to know the suffering and only then the joy of coming to respond to his love.[11]

The 'Antiochene' answer, and its modern variants, are unable to express what I want to say. But that still leaves me with the problem of finding some other way of talking of God 'being' a man: foetus, baby, boy, and adult.

The traditional alternative is the sort of answer that theologians from Alexandria tended to produce (the line that proved attractive to Austen and Rudi on our jury).[12]

In the first place, you allow for distinctions within the

life and being of God. A modern form of this view would allow that 'God' is a community of three persons linked indissolubly by the love between them. Then it is suggested that only one of these three 'persons' (in an old or modern sense of 'person') is made man as Jesus of Nazareth: 'the Son', 'the Word'. It then becomes necessary to avoid the charge of splitting God up; but this approach does lessen the embarrassment a little. The entirety of God is not now supposed to have been withdrawn from the activity of preserving the world in being. Only the Son in the community of God is made man.

A version of this part of the traditional Alexandrian 'myth' I find necessary. The other part of the Alexandrian answer I find much less satisfactory. The Alexandrian theologians went on to add that the Son, the person of God who was made man, could not, of course, really be limited by this act, and must have absorbed, as it were, the manhood, the humanness of Jesus, so that little or nothing distinctively human remained.

The trouble was that neither the Antiochene nor the Alexandrian theologians – nor many of their present-day successors, for that matter – were willing to allow their understanding of God to be at all drastically – or drastically enough – modified by what they knew of Jesus the Christ. For both, God the Son (as much as God the Father) is 'impassible', 'infinite'; he is, to be honest, that which cannot (by definition cannot) be limited by space, time, experience. He is that which by definition *cannot* be man. Trying to say that he was man, was 'incarnate', obviously imposed a considerable strain. Antioch lessened the strain by loosing the tie of God the Son with Jesus the man; Alexandria by minimizing the manliness of the man God was believed to have been tied to. Either way, the humble service of God to men in which I wish to believe disappears in the pretence of a half-hearted incarnation. The Council of Chalcedon which tried to mediate between the two views could find no satisfactory third possibility, and just added together a mild form of each.

But if I am to believe that God is love, I must believe that he is free to suffer. I must believe in the essential 'humanity' of God. I must believe, if I may put it this way, that he is great enough to be able and willing to accept human limitations for the furtherance of love.[13]

It may still be a problem to decide how it may be said that the 'eternal Son of God' played his part in the creative sustaining of the universe while a man. But I find it easy to suppose that he found a simple, if costly, solution. I find I can and must believe that 'the Son', one of the three persons of the community of God, was free and willing to 'be' Jesus; and, as Jesus, was fully involved in the pain and joy of loving men and women in first-century Palestine. This I must believe, because only so will my 'myth' demand and elicit the commitment I wish to make.

## (v) God unawares

I have still not answered one of my earlier questions. Even allowing that God the Son (as I understand him) could 'be' Jesus, how can he in any sense have 'been' Jesus without Jesus knowing it? The synoptic record, as I read it, suggests that Jesus said he was not good as God is good. Jesus would have preferred not to do God's will in Jerusalem. Mark tells us that Jesus took his crucifixion as God's rejection of him. He had thought that God's rule would be effective soon, perhaps in his own lifetime, and obviously he was wrong. I have already said that I cannot accept as authentic

65

any explicit or even implied claim to godhead on Jesus' part. So far as his conscious – and, presumably, unconscious – mind went, Jesus was just a man.

In terms of the most common version of the Christian 'myth', even in his personal relation to the God he called Father, Jesus (I would say) was just a man. He was enabled, guided, led by 'the Holy Spirit', the third 'person' of the community of God. He was the area where 'the paradox of the grace of God' happened as fully as then it might: the paradox of the power that overwhelms you and in over-whelming you sets you free to be supremely yourself in your loving and caring. Jesus was a man who found he could live as God then would have him live. By the Spirit of God, Jesus was obedient to the will of the Father as and where he knew it. That is all. (But I would hope that would make sense to Nesta, on my imaginary jury.)[14]

'By the Spirit of God' is the key phrase (and a phrase to which contemporary discussion of traditional theology has not paid sufficient attention). In his relation to God by the Spirit, Jesus lived a human life, was no less, but no more, than a saint. *But by his relation to the Son*, the Word of God, Jesus was quite unique.[15]

Much of the contemporary debate about Jesus and God has unnecessarily starved itself of terms which the tradition supplies. It has supposed that the only way to maintain a belief in Jesus as a real man is to make his relation to the Word of God, the second person of God, the relationship of any ordinary man enhanced to a unique degree. What I am suggesting is that it makes more sense of the tradition (and certainly better fits the commitment in trust that I wish to make) to allow that in his relation to God through the Spirit, Jesus was quite an ordinary man. But in his relation to God the Son, Jesus has no parallel.

66

There is then no unreality in this understanding of Christ. He is a total physical organism, brain, brawn, bowels, and bladder. There is no metaphysical 'part' – soul, spirit, mind, heart, will – to be replaced by some indwelling aspect of deity. Empirically, this view would allow him to have been what the records, read critically, suggest: just another man. There is nothing to make him different in himself from other men, more or less than a man.

But at the same time, in the love of the Trinity, the three-person community of God, Jesus is God. The Son, I must believe, was accepting as his own every experience, every action and sensation of that physical organism, Jesus; and not as an observer, but as a subject (a co-subject) of all that was done by or happened to that fully personal Jesus. (I would expect the pattern of 'the Son' immersed in the life of Jesus to ring a bell with Austen.) This was God, accepting the dreaming innocence of the womb, the anguish of birth, the pain of separation, and coming to self-consciousness. God the Son was accepting ignorance and hunger and the flavour of bread baked on the hearth, the excitement of wine at village parties. He was battered by social conditioning, by the urge to pride and hatred, to cruelty, callousness, self-righteousness, narrow sectarianisms. This was God, torn by the pain of love limited in what it can achieve, the pain of seeing for now nothing of the ultimate possibilities of love and freedom. This was God, taking all that came the way of the human organism Jesus, with no pretence, no protection. The love was the love of an ordinary sensual man, the pain was the pain of ordinary nerves and brain. (But the commitment of the Son to Jesus, and of Jesus to the Father may be deep enough to inspire confidence even in Rudi.)

This was God. Jesus was God, without knowing it, because God was Jesus by deliberate choice, commitment, acceptance. God bled, God let his mind be torn to shreds by pain, to reconcile his world to him, to be part of the pain that his love had seen good to let his world suffer. God accepted the pain and joy of a man who loved as well, it seems, as any ordinary man has loved.

Popular Christianity has always wanted to say things like this (compare the Christmas and Passiontide and Easter hymns and carols); its sophisticated theologians have always been afraid to. From the days of the evangelist John they have been unwilling to admit what they could only half believe was true, that the God they were committed to was a man who lived and died.

Does this really allow me to say that God 'was' Jesus, that Jesus 'was' God? For me, 'identity', 'self' means the sum total of mentally recorded and consciously or subconsciously effective past active and passive experiences and inherited traits. If this is shared, then so is identity. Identity, in the sense of 'numerical identity', by definition cannot be shared; but in this abstract sense it is unimportant in human relationships.[16]

# (vi) Concluding

I have suggested a variant of the Christian 'myth' that has close links with dogmatic orthodoxy. It might even look like an attempt to spell out the traditional belief that Jesus has two 'natures', human and divine, in the one *prosopon* (one outward expression), without using those particular philosophical terms. My view has, as I have mentioned, even closer links with popular 'orthodoxy', which insists on calling Jesus 'God', despite the frowns of some theologians:

Our God, heaven cannot hold him
   Nor earth sustain;
Heaven and earth shall flee away
   When he comes to reign:
In the bleak mid-winter
   A stable-place sufficed
The Lord God Almighty,
   Jesus Christ.[17]

Or earlier,

Then why, O blessèd Jesu Christ,
   Should I not love thee well?
Not for the sake of winning heaven,
   Or of escaping hell; . . .

E'en so I love thee, and will love,
   And in thy praise will sing,
Solely because thou art my God,
   And my eternal King.[18]

It is dependent on Trinitarian theology, but again refuses the technical terms (*hypostasis/persona* and *ousia/substantia*). It is not orthodox by technical standards (which seek to tie the theologian to a dated terminology and ways of thinking). But its 'radical' intention is none the less to be more 'orthodox' than orthodoxy can now appear. (This has to be so, whenever there is a 'new reformation'.)

Of course, if you want Christianity to provide you with objective knowledge of God, then my view will not help you. I do not know what will; but you may. If you want a comprehensive scheme of meaning for the world, the understanding of Christian faith that I offer will seem too subjective. I do not want such 'objective' knowledge, such a 'scheme of meaning'; and I do not think they are to be had. I want, and here I have outlined, a 'myth' as a form of ethical commitment: a myth that allows me to talk of the love and humility and freedom of God, allows me to strive for them, allows me to hope I may be brought to them, allows me to be grateful if ever I approach them.

By their fruits we are to know them. Dogmas and myths are included in the test. It is this test that has driven me to this critique and formulation. And a statement in terms of a 'logic of love' must be tested by the love it focuses and makes articulate. Do we, do I, obey, love, serve in freedom Jesus as Lord? Then whatever words are used are good enough. If there is no love, service, obedience, freedom, then there are no words strong enough to make Jesus a living Lord, to make him God.

So the question stands: Can we share his freedom and service and love, so that he is our God? Can you, will you, so that he is yours?

I have my own vote, of course, and I have hopes for the decisions of three members of my imaginary jury. The decisions of the other members will always have to wait till they see what happens. Their decision depends on yours as well as mine. How do we respond?

# 5. The God for You?

IT CAN seem intolerably arrogant to claim that 'my' God is yours, and should be accepted by you. Unless, that is, I can somehow prove my case objectively. The scientist who claims that everyone else is wrong may seem arrogant (and may be arrogant); but at least he will demonstrate the steps that led to his disturbing conclusions, and give others the chance to repeat his experiments (and even prove him wrong). I have only elaborated a way of looking at life for the living of it that takes my serious fancy. What right have I to attempt to foist this on anyone else? If I were a poet, it might be allowed. But my writing has no real claim to be read for its beauty. And people have usually written 'theology' as though it were a matter of 'truth', the most important possible truth, not an individual fancy. I too have said that I must fancy that my God is real apart from my imagining him – that I am real, even, only because he imagines me – even though I admit that my only clues to him are ideas of others and ideas of my own that capture my imagination and will. This does seem to need some further justification.

## (i) The uncertain scientist and the obliging model

Scientists used to believe that what they said about the structure of the physical universe was literally true in a very simple and direct way, so that it amounted to a series of 'laws that never could be broken'. They supposed that their general pictures of how things work were like photographs in words. The sequence of cause and effect, for instance, was like a very complicated game of billiards. If at some point you knew the position, direction, and velocity of all the balls – all the atoms – you could in theory work out accurately everything that would ever happen afterwards. Your billiard-table picture gave you an objectively true picture of the universe. (Maybe some still believe this.) And by comparison, of course, talk of God has seemed vague, imprecise, useless.

This confidence of the scientists has broken down. In part it has been because the pictures keep having to be replaced. 'Phlogiston' had to be abandoned; and the interstellar ether. It became necessary, for instance, to use two contradictory pictures for the activity of the most basic 'items' discovered to date. In one way they seemed to act as though they were particles with mass, etc.; in another way, they seemed to act like waves, light waves, etc.; and the 'billiard table' was not good enough. No one could find a single consistent picture that fitted what had been found. Of course, this might just have led the scientists to go on hoping that, in the end, someone might think up a good picture; or someone might see things more clearly, so that they could be clearly expressed in one final picture, true for all time. But it has become fairly obvious that this is not very likely to happen.[1]

It became obvious because it was realized that when an investigator started to examine part of the world around him, just the fact that he was investigating had some effect on what he was examining. Looking at a mountain does not have much noticeable effect on the mountain. Looking an elephant in the eye may have some considerable effect on the elephant (and the investigator). 'Looking at' a wave-particle changes its behaviour to a considerable extent. You will see it differently, depending on which aspect of its behaviour you are concentrating on. And whatever means you use to isolate it for observation will alter the way it would otherwise behave. You can only record its behaviour when it is being bombarded, or otherwise interfered with. You have to 'catch' it to take note of it; you can never observe it when it is not affected by being observed. You will make what seems to you the best apparatus for record-ing its behaviour – that apparatus will change its behaviour in some ways; another apparatus would change it in other ways – and so what you think it is likely to do will shape what in the end you see. Another man with a different theory to test will make his wave-particles dance, at least in part, to his tune; and that is what he will see. It does not mean that they will dance to just any tune. But it makes it very hard to show that any one tune, hypothesis, picture, 'model', is the one and only true one. You do not make a 'scientific law'; you ask, 'Will this hypothesis, this "model" work, on balance, in this situation – will it work, will it help me to "see" what is happening, co-ordinate my investigation and then my findings?'

And thirdly, quite a lot of philosophers (again, maybe not all) have suggested that the only sure and certain statements are those that go round in a circle. In ordinary mathematics, two and two make four because that is what 'two', 'and', 'make', 'four' mean. It was decided before you started. It is true and always will be because it is rigged that way. In men's memory, the sun has always 'risen'. That does not 'prove' it will tomorrow (though it is very, very likely). 'The sun will rise tomorrow' is not sure in the same way that 'two and two will make four tomorrow' is sure.[2]

The researcher uses word-models that have worked before, and work that has come out of others' use of good and not-so-good models; and maybe makes fresh word-models to help him sort out in advance what to look for. They may work well. In that case they are useful. But in the end they may break down, because of the fresh evidence they help him or someone else to find. Or because of his or someone else's work with a quite different model.

I have talked in terms of physics. But a sociologist, for instance, uses models too. Sometimes he looks at groups of people and individuals as though they were machines and machine-parts. Other times, he looks at them as though they were organisms and limbs or cells. (And different types of machine and different kinds of organism.) This helps him to collect a manageable list of findings, and appreciate what he finds. It does not prove that human societies are machines, or vast organisms. These models are devices for finding things out. They help you act as researcher.[3]

When the scientist thus becomes more hesitant in his approach and thinking, the believer and the theologian may (I stress *may*) suffer less by comparison.

74

# (ii) The working model

A politician may use models rather differently. He may look at one of his party's research team's reports, and say, 'Ah, society can be looked at like a machine. That makes sense to me.' (Or he may just like machines and ignore the research.) 'I think it *should* work like an efficient machine. No fancy bits; anything that does not contribute to the work must be scrapped. No Victorian wrought-iron and engraving in this mechanism!' And another politician may also look at some research (or just guess) and say, 'Society should work like a living organism. We know that seemingly useless bits can often turn out to be essential to the continuing life of the whole body.'

These are not so much models to help you find out things; they are models for action, models to guide you in constructing something that you have in hand. Of course, they may lead to your finding things out. You may find that your carefully constructed social machine rebels in a very un-machinelike way, and changes its own shape, and still moves, and is more like an adaptable organism. Your free organism may just refuse to grow, and, instead, settle down into a mechanical repetition of functions; with the politician unable to let any part care organically for itself, but having to dart around like a mechanic with grease-gun and spare parts. The two different uses for models, the finding out and the constructional uses, are different; but they do overlap.

And most, if not all, human beings have a model or models for thinking and living out their lives. Often they are not aware of it; and even if they are, they may think and work with the help of very different, even contradictory models. But they have them; and the discussion of them that we have just been through is partly to show what models are like and can be used for, and to show (if that matters to you) that they are very much in place in this 'modern' and scientific and technological age.

A man may live by a very simple form of nineteenth-century biologist's model, 'Nature red in tooth and claw', 'the survival of the fittest' – by which he may mean the survival of the biggest and strongest and most brutal. Or he may live by a more recent and biologically more useful model, the survival of the most adaptable – the most able to adapt himself and his surroundings. He may have one model for use at home: the Victorian-Roman father of a family, leader of men, conservative, traditionalist; and another for the place where he works: the free-thinking lonely explorer, fending for himself, responsible for none and to none; and another at his club, where he is one of a herd, doing what the shapeless mass does, with no one standing out; while in his car he is a knight in shining armour, fighting for the approval of the woman who rides with him; and so on.

Someone else may feel that this man's models are very inefficient, running him into considerable trouble, just not enabling him to do what he really consciously wants to. The father-figure model may not work at all at home; if he tried it at work, it might 'work' very much better than the 'lonely explorer' one. But suppose you show him that this could well be true. He may say, 'But I just do not want the sort of success that would come from being a father-figure at work; I would much rather fail at work, if fail I must, as the pioneering individual I admire in that setting.' Some models may work much more easily than others. But he may prefer to try to make a very difficult model work. And I, at least, cannot see a way to prove that he is 'wrong'. His model may not fit the facts: he may want to make the facts fit the model. After all, that is what his model is for. It is a basis for making something new – like a flying machine that is 'impossible' because heavier than air; or a community where people become less self-centred.

A more reflective sort of person may have models of the 'finding out' sort, alongside, or also doing duty as, 'working' models. Not quite the same as the 'billiard-table' or the 'waves-and-particles'; but as ways of trying to understand the world and human life as a whole. Is it like a home in which children are loved and grow; or a school; or a competitive game; or a battlefield; or a poisonous bog, inescapably destructive; or a brothel; or an art gallery; or a combination of these? And he could decide that it was 'really' like a school, but he was going to treat it like a rugby scrum; really a foul, heaving morass, but he was going to try to make it a home, even though he was bound to lose. The two types of model may marry, but they do not have to (only they cannot help having some effect on each other).

Again, it is extremely difficult to prove to someone that his total picture is wrong. It is so much bound up with his own present experience, or childhood, or later life: was it kindly, cruel, enervating, stifling, stimulating? and so on. Here, even more than for the scientist, with his very limited models, the way you use your model to focus on the evidence determines very much what counts as evidence, and determines the way you see the evidence that your model tells you is relevant. Of course, if you see the world as a class-room or a laboratory or a controlled experiment, you may feel quite sure that its 'meaning' can and must be demonstrated. Your model will make you see your model as 'true', or as pointing to the truth; and others as false. Another man may feel that he can show that your model is inadequate, without having to fall in with your model's mood, by trying in any way to 'prove' some alternative.

Plainly, models for living provide an attractive setting for the believer's talk of Jesus and God.

# (iii) Jesus and God and models for living

Christian Churches can provide you with a variety of models. Jesus himself invites you to see yourself and your world (as we have noticed) as a place where a selfish fool can be accepted home – or expelled. As a party, but also as a court-house; as a rigid stock exchange, and as a utopia where every need is met, and no one can be redundant. The Churches present you with varying pictures of Jesus himself as a more complex model, his whole life and his teaching, his death and resurrection, as a model for what all life is for, and how it is to be lived. Later theology develops and amplifies the models in different situations for different purposes. Each Church has variants of common models, and also quite distinct models; and certainly between the Churches the models can conflict and be diametrically opposed at points, even very important ones.

Christology, the discussion of Christ, may be the focal point of the main complex model; or it may be just the most important perspective, or even just one perspective by which to view the centre of one model among many. I am offering a briefly worked out view of Jesus as the focal point of a complex and embracing model for life: a life in which Jesus is your God, and you share his freedom.

Christians differ as to whether their models are primarily 'meaning' models (which may have implications for action); or whether they are primarily 'action' models (which may none the less suggest overall purpose and so meaning). Which way you see your model is itself part of your model. Which way you see Jesus' or the Churches' traditional intentions will be affected by your model. The chances are that if you see Jesus' purpose in terms of a 'meaning' model, you will see him as 'revealer' (*the* Relevation of God). If you see him in terms of an action model, he is 'redeemer', 'saviour', the one who sets you free to be like him. But the two often overlap. If you see him as giving 'meaning', you may feel that you can prove that other models (including other versions of Christ-model) are 'wrong' and yours 'right'. (But not everyone who takes the meaning line supposes that.) If you see him as affording a (powerful) model for action, you may (as in my case) not find it useful to attempt to 'prove' anything: except by action. 'You will know them by their fruits.' And action, as I shall suggest, remains ambiguous. (Of course, in my view, Jesus sees himself in 'action' terms, primarily. A lot of later theology turns him into primarily a 'meaning' model, and one that can be proved, or is part of a whole that can be proved. So, for many people, 'theology' has become the implausible proof of purposeless meanings.)*

## (iv) 'Is' and 'ought', 'meaning' and 'working'

The distinction that I am drawing between a general 'meaning' model and a general 'working' model is similar to the distinction which many philosophers draw between factual assertions and moral assertions, between 'is' and 'ought'. Two people can be completely agreed as to the facts of a situation, the possible courses of action, the likely results: and still disagree entirely on what 'ought' to be done. Of two twins, agreed on the facts, one says, 'No, Dad, you ought to put Gran before Mother'; and the other, 'No, you ought to put Mother before Gran.' They are aware of their own and each other's psychological motivations. There are no further available facts. They just disagree about what should be done. Or take the same two twins and their motor-car. They both know it is made to travel safely at speeds up to 85 miles an hour, they know about the controls, and road holding; road laws, and road dangers. One says you ought to travel at the same speed as other traffic, even if that means breaking the limit; the other says you should not. (They both accept, for instance, that driving at 30 on a broad but restricted road may infuriate other motorists.) They know what the car and the road and the signs are for; they do not agree how they should act. Two scientists can make a hydrogen bomb, they know the effect of exploding it in a centre of population; they even agree on the likely deterrent effect of their country possessing it. One thinks it should possess it, the other that it should not.[5]

Is talk about Jesus and God like talk about what a car is for, what the known rules of the road are, how you can escape prosecution, 'what the facts are'? Or is it more a discussion of what we ought to do? 'the true meaning' that might be proved or 'the right action' that cannot? 'meaning model' or 'working model'?

We have already noted that some, maybe many, take all their beliefs about Jesus and God as 'factually' true, assertions that can be proved, to any but a fool. I have suggested, on the other hand, that this talk about Jesus and God is at least primarily talk about how we 'ought' to behave in our world, and have defended that. Certainly, the amount of disagreement about God and Jesus suggests that the debate is not about 'what factually is the case' (in any ordinary sense of the terms) but about 'what ought to be'.

Of course, to be fair, it is possible for experts to disagree for ages about 'the facts' (disagreement does not immediately prove that they are not discussing facts). But at least they will usually agree about how 'the facts' should be found. And people with very different views about 'what ought to be' do none the less often have very close agreement about 'what is the case now'. (Someone may insist on talking about 'moral facts' or 'theological facts' – but that still leaves the difficulty of finding how to establish them; they are still different from 'empirical', testable facts.) The amount of disagreement in theological debate makes it look most like a debate about 'what ought to be.'

Having made this distinction between 'is' and 'ought' I must add an important qualification. What looks at first sight like a 'factual' assertion may carry with it a larger or smaller load of insistence on what ought to be done. 'There is a step here', seems purely factual. But the architect, pointing to it on the plan, may be instructing the builder, the estate agent may be warning his client, and so on. If, though, there is not a step there, the implicit directions for action disappear completely. On the other hand, 'You ought to watch your step' *can* be meaningful even in the absence of any factual information about actual hazards. But even this would lose meaning if there were never any relevant factual considerations concerning perambulation, literal or metaphorical. 'Is'-type statements may have undertones of 'ought'. 'Ought'-type assertions must have at least a context of fact. ('Ought' implies 'can'.)

So we have to maintain the theoretical distinction between 'is' and 'ought', and that between general 'meaning' models and general 'working' models, while accepting that in practice probably neither can ever be found in an entirely 'pure' form. Much that you find yourself saying will contain a mixture of both, even if one side is represented only by the merest trace. And still, in any mixture, the 'facts' are what can be tested, demonstrated, even 'proved'; the morality, the 'ought', is what may be agreed but cannot be proved to be right.⁶

I do not suppose that I have 'proved' this position, over against the man who is sure that he can 'prove', or that someone could 'prove', what is the truth about God and Jesus and the meaning of the world and the one right way to act in it. I cannot disprove that view, because I do not know what could possibly count as proof of it. I can only offer you, as a working model, a picture of Jesus the Christ, the second person of the triune God; in the picture, facts about Jesus, men, and the world are relevant; but it is predominantly meant as a strong and supple empowering and enliberating pattern for action to change the world, and so, but only so, to help interpret the world. I can try to establish the relevant facts; but I can then only offer the whole for you to take it more – or less – whole; or reject it. I can only offer it, not prove it. It is that kind of model.

The model may be compelling to you, it may be absurd. All I hope to have done in this chapter so far is to have shown that to sketch out and offer such a model is itself a useful and intelligible activity. I suggest, at least, that in questions of Jesus and God and the world and man this is all that can be done. To offer 'my' vision, my model, may seem objectionably egotistical – 'I', 'me', 'my', all the time. But to take the other line, and say that mine is the objective truth before which I humbly bow, true whether I like it or not, is to call everyone who disagrees with me either a fool or a knave for not accepting the plain truth before his eyes. There is greater arrogance in this latter show of humility (and not a little idolatry). It is only when we stop trying to 'prove' our theological positions, for and against, and

instead, discuss them, and live them to the full, that progress
may come.

## (v) 'Concern for persons' and the last hope for proof

We have to disagree with Anselm, Aquinas, and the church
bookcase tracts with their attempts to prove – Anselm,
from the way things seem to be, Aquinas, from the way
things seem to happen – though many people still find
these attempts useful, as offering to us highly developed
forms of Christian model. If you want, in a Christian way,
to have your view of the world included within your view
of God, then your understanding of God will have to
stretch your imagination to its outer limits, further than
any other theme can take it (Anselm). And everything that
has ever happened in the world or that ever may will have
to point you to your God. Where things work efficiently
and smoothly together, you can expect to live by your
model; rather than in chaos, confusion, and 'miraculous'
irregularity (Aquinas). Aquinas, Anselm, Descartes, Paley
and Co. tried to prove God; for most men, at least today,
they do not succeed in proving even that we must have a
theistic model at all, still less that theirs is the best theistic
model available. But they are a useful part of the inherited
craft of model-making, and we can learn from them if we
are going to build that type of model.[7]

Perhaps the philosopher Immanuel Kant was on to a
better bet when he tried to show that God was an essential
background and frame for an ethical model, a model for
looking at how things 'ought' to be. In a way, my last
chapter tried to do that: tried to show that some form or

forms of Christian way of life, of behaviour towards other men, need a 'model' that refers to God who powerfully loves and accepts. Kant's was a different God for a different ethical model. But if I am right in some of my earlier suggestions, for many people, talk of God fits best 'into' (for some), or 'around' (for others), talk of 'what ought to be'.

Is it not possible to find something which a very wide range of people think 'ought to be', and then see if that does not demand a wider, maybe even a theistic ('God-centred') model, for its proper appreciation – and execution? It is no use looking at 'the family', or 'marriage', or 'property', or 'the preservation of physical life' even. At least, these are not very promising, because people take such different views of them. But perhaps some wider view of 'what ought to be' might provide a basis.

In his Bampton Lectures for 1966, David Jenkins suggests just such a general starting point for 'the debate about God'. 'I assume one ground which I take to be self-evident, universal, and inescapable. I assume that our concern is with persons.' And he goes on to say that at this point 'fact' and 'value' coincide (or at least largely overlap). We have already noticed that in practice it is possible for 'is' and 'ought' to be closely intertwined. David Jenkins suggests that here they cannot properly be even theoretically distinguished. If this is so, then the basis in fact should make a very good agreed foundation; while the basis in value would seem likely to afford the Christian an excellent opportunity to show the usefulness – even the necessity – of his talk about God.

For his defence of his claim – 'every human being is under a compulsion, *both factual and moral*, to be concerned with persons' – I refer you to David Jenkins's book. It continues to be relevant for our case. He argues that this concern for

84

persons stems in fact from Jesus and the debate about Jesus' significance in the first five centuries of the Church's life. And he argues further that *only* a continuing concentration on the things concerning Jesus and God can allow man's personalness to develop. Otherwise it will be destroyed by a concern for things (science) that ignores personalness, or by an escape from things (mysticism, Zen) that is also an escape from personalness, or by despair (in existentialism: whether it takes the form of nausea or hopeless defiance). The 'death of God' means the death of man.[8]

This seems to me the most persuasive attempt I have yet met to demonstrate from agreed ground the need for a Christian model for life in the world. And for all the attempt to demonstrate, it is open, flexible, tentative. But I cannot see any *logical* necessity in the position (even given the analysis of the historical origins of the concern for personalness). Maybe it did begin here; that does not show that it cannot continue independently. Agreed, there may be strong threats to personalness, in the modern world: from scientism, withdrawal to Zen or LSD, or sick or courageous despair. This may be particularly obvious in academic, literary, and theatrical circles. But it is a question of fact. If concern for persons is factual, it demands factual investigation. For the present I do not feel that concern for persons is markedly absent in all non-Christian groups; nor, sadly, markedly enhanced in all Christian ones. Jenkins's analysis may turn out to be a true prophecy. It cannot yet be shown that for those for whom God (and Christ) are dead beyond interest the death of personalness is inevitable.

There is a striking similarity between David Jenkins's approach and that of the American Jewish philosopher, Abraham J. Heschel in, for instance, *Who is Man?* He too says that where persons are concerned, fact and value cannot be distinguished. He conveys the same sense of

85

man's personal existence being threatened, and by the same forces. There is the same protest against the 'Cartesian' division of man's world, which divides him. There is the same insistence that the answer to the question about man lies with God (who asked it). But for Heschel, of course, the source of the concern, and the answer, stems from Judaic theism; in contrast to Jenkins's, from Christian theism. So even if the common ground of personalness is chosen, it is not easy to show that Jesus the Christ is even a necessary point of reference.[9]

What the two books do show, however, is that concern for persons is a good basis for debate, because it may well be shared. But we are left without proof, and I can only continue to try to share 'my' vision (just as others have shared theirs with me).

Jenkins says, towards the end of his final chapter;

> But, it may be urged, all this is only a vision, a possible perspective, a personal hope. So it is. But it is a vision which has strong claims to have elements of true insight arising from the givenness of Jesus Christ rooted in materiality and events, arising also from the observed givenness of personalness and renewed in the continually experienced givenness of the possibilities which arise out of and in connection with the worship of God.

But it is a vision.

## (vi) There can be no certainty

In another book, I have argued that the one certain thing for a Christian today is that he can have no Christian certainty. He has no clarity, nothing settled and established and provable. To be sure, then and now I admit that it is possible to wrest from the world and God a sort of make-believe certainty. If you settle down into some small sect, of strict brethren, or of liberal modernists, or of any other kind, the unanimity of your restricted circle may look like a clear certainty revealed from heaven. But if you accept a wide range of Christians as your companions in faith they are your companions in an unclear faith that is riddled with contradictions, set at cross-purposes, unable to come to a common mind on the structure of a comprehensive Christian model and its implications for living.[10]

Is this in any way tolerable, this uncertainty? The Churches lose members to the sects at least in part because they fail to offer a faith that is clear-cut and unambiguous. Religion is 'the balm of life, the cure of woe', 'soothes your sorrows, heals your wounds, and drives away your fear'; 'our heart is restless till it rests in God'. And so on. This is what some have said they look for in 'religion' and 'faith'.

So it may be that trust such as I have talked of makes an intolerable demand. But it is a demand that human beings have to face. (I raised this point briefly in the previous chapter.) When two people get married – according to the Anglican rite, which is much the same as many others – they make just this sort of commitment to each other. The chances are they do not know each other all that well, anyway, even at the time. They certainly do not know what each other – or each self – is going to become. And they say, 'Come what may, I'm yours.' For better for worse: external circumstances, and the play of inter-personal relations. It is a deliberate unconditional commitment.

Of course it can break down into suspicion, rancour, hate. But while it works, they give and receive something like a complete trust. Love giving and returning love can do no less, demand no less. Once conditions come in ('so much licence, so much suspect behaviour, then out'), anything like a fullness of love vanishes.

And it is this sort of trust, I suggest, that God demands. (Or you could put it, 'There have long been versions of the Jewish-Christian theistic model which have insisted on this depth of commitment.') Abraham is its first focus: to leave home and security for the vision of something beyond dreaming, too old for an heir (and asked to sacrifice first the makeshift and then the real successor), able to receive in the promised land only a tomb. Job, secure in society, secure in the rightness of his benevolent way of life, shattered, and then still trusting a God he could only abuse. His friends say, 'Settle back into the security of the orthodox position, get back into control of the situation by centring it on your own sin and guilt, your own responsibility, so that your own penitence can straighten it all out.' But Job insists on the agonizing uncertainty of his faith.

'My God, my God, why have you forsaken me?' is thought by some scholars to be just a cue-line for reading the whole of Psalm 22, which portrays triumph after suffering and humiliation. But there is everything to suggest that for Jesus death, strung up on a Roman gibbet, would be the sign of God's abandonment in a much more objective way than any agony of pain and mental breakdown. The cry may be an interpretative addition, but it is a valid one. The man who is at the heart of God's purpose for the world accepts this sort of uncertainty at God's hands. (Or you could put it, 'At the centre of our model for life in our world stands this symbol of shattered faith.')

Eastern Christian theologians have long been used to accepting forms of this uncertainty. In the end, they say, theology has to be negative; you doubt everything, even the heart and centre of your model itself: because the model with which you start demands that you face this final insecurity. In the West too, mystics have found this must be met. St John of the Cross, for instance; or English writers such as the author of *The Cloud of Unknowing*, or Walter Hilton, or Julian of Norwich. All certainty in Christian faith leaves you, all joy in believing, in worship, sacraments, prayer, fellowship, disappears; you are left alone, drear, just trusting the God who has gone: the model that has fallen apart in your hands.[11]

Western theologians have mostly wanted everything much tidier, clear-cut, with a neat legal precision that would allow you to codify laws about heresy; or at least be certain yourself. Even some of the Christian thinkers who have done most to shake the complacency of their western fellow believers have really been trying to reduce the Christian model, Christian faith, to a few points that would be secure, that even they could not disturb. Sören Kierkegaard, Paul Tillich, Rudolf Bultmann, in England Bishop John Robinson, have tried to modify their 'model' so that science, psychology, philosophy, and so on, will not touch it; and what is left will be clear and secure. But God seems to demand (or you could put it, 'accepting a comprehensive Christian model seems to entail') a continuous risk at every point.

Everything has to be questioned. The model insists on focusing attention on a man it says really lived: so you have to cross-examine the witnesses, again and again, to find the truth about this man – and risk finding there is nothing to say, or only unhappy things to say. The model insists you believe that God is real: but how can you say that, even to yourself? is there any sense in it at all? And is the model just the product of the sickness of my mind? or worse – of my guilt and pride? And the love which this model has allowed you to glimpse is such that you have to risk all this and more for it. If you do not take the risk, you have anyway already lost. If the risk is not worth it, there is no God worth trusting.

(Or you could put it, 'The ultimate test of a model for the whole of life: can you, as you hope, use it, and consistently, as a model for action, when it has ceased to function as a model for meaning?')

Accepting this overall uncertainty means that you can face the whole host of lesser uncertainties with much greater equanimity and openness. With this ultimate faith in God (or you could put it, 'accepting the ultimate demands of the Jewish-Christian – and to some extent Platonic – theistic model') it is possible to face the questions that arise with a certain increase in objectivity. You can follow a trail wherever it leads. Of course, it may shatter your faith. But there is no longer any logical necessity in that; because there is nothing you cannot be led to question, nothing of which the questioning would have to mean the collapse of everything. With this sort of faith, you are free.

I suppose most human beings want some sort of security. So I offer this paradox of commitment: 'In abandoning any ready-made defences, at last you are nakedly secure.' 'Unless you become as a little child . . .'

But, of course, little children only trust their parents because, and for as long as, they keep them physically and psychologically comfortable. They very largely misunderstand their parents, insist on their playing a role that fits a child's needs. Only in adult life will they come to accept their parents for what they really are, rather than the ideal figures they have projected on to them, providers of comfort and security. The later, 'truer' relationship may come only through pain and disillusion; and it will always have its base in early false impressions. But the truer relation holds a far richer promise, even if it does only come through the shattering of all that was first accepted.

If God is real, if Jesus is real, as the model invites you to believe, then you can only reach the real Jesus and the real God through the questioning of every accepted position, because Jesus and God are greater still. Everything must be able to be questioned and shattered, in case it prove to be standing in the way of the Love you just glimpsed through it, and which you must reach beyond it. There is no place to build, and hardly room to stand still, until you are lost – and found – in the magnificent uncertainty and openness of God's sure love.

This sort of paradox can be headily exciting, or infuriating and repellent. The question that must be asked is, Does it work? Can you live by this model? and what effect may it have, does it have?

Maybe you have already been attracted for far longer than I have by God, in ways similar enough to those I have been talking about, with similar emphases and qualifications. Perhaps you have even been a bit attracted by what I have written, so that it does become at least an interesting possibility in a way like this to accept Jesus as God. How does this 'Christological' model work in practice? What 'style of life' can be expected to follow?

# 6.   The Man for You?[1]

## (i) Freedom and the man Jesus

IT IS possible for you to share Jesus' freedom and openness for other people and for God in the world around. This is what at least some believers have found. Of course, they have not always put it that way; but it has some appeal to some of my contemporaries, and to me. It is possible to share Jesus' freedom: his freedom for men, his freedom for his God.

'Freedom' is a confusing word. Like 'democracy', lots of people claim it. With so many conflicting uses, 'democracy' seems to have no meaning. But with 'freedom' you are necessarily free to give it what meaning you will.

One man's liberty is another man's prison. If the society in which you are set makes you free to be a capitalist, it denies you the freedom to live as a Marxist; it may through the dead weight of public opinion even deny you the freedom to consider Marxism as a possibility.

A man may long for the freedom to live secure in a prison cell; and the judge may condemn him to a captive torture in the relentless demanding world outside. One man's liberty is another man's prison.

Still, for most, life chained to a prison wall is not free. Unchained in the cell, you are freer; once through the door into the prison yard, you are freer still. You have a wider and wider range of possibilities open to you; you have less and less 'external' compulsion.

Chained side by side are two men. For both, movement and space are an urgent need. One has a vivid and ranging imagination. 'Stone walls do not a prison make, Nor iron bars a cage', he says, and has a greater freedom than his companion. 'No, but they make a ruddy good imitation.' Offer to release them; but the prisoner with the dangerous gift of imagination must agree to brain surgery and the loss of this magic. Which freedom should he choose?

It is only a temporary choice, anyway. The iron would eat into his soul, the chains in the end would drag down his dancing visions. For most men, the basic freedoms, the ones to fight for, the ones which allow you to enjoy the others, are the freedom to have a full belly, a good sleep every twenty-four hours, a place to call your own, people to call your own (and a job, if that is the only way to find your place among people). Then you can start to worry about the range of your ideas and dreams and visions, music, poetry, pictures, travel, enjoying your own or others' creativity.

There's the rub. If freedom could just be dreams, my neighbour and I could roam freely without ever trespassing, without ever cutting short each other's adventure. But if there is only room for one of us to lie down and sleep, then only one of us is free to dream his dream undisturbed to its end. If only a living man can dream and only an eating,

93

drinking, breathing man can live; and if I exercise my freedom to eat twice what I need, I deny to my starving neighbour the freedom even to dream again.

My freedom threatens my neighbour's; my neighbour's freedom threatens mine. So we have laws, to keep the threat from developing too far. The protecting of my freedom curtails his – and mine. Freedom is relative; freedom is never 'FREEDOM', just like that. It is freedom from that, freedom for this.

And the greatest brake on my freedom is me. To much of the world, and even to myself, I may seem free. A never-ending range of people and places and things to surround myself with, the very minimum of external compulsion. A law to myself, I say. And that is a law that I may find it very hard to break free of. I am bound by my own past. The genetic pattern, the reaction to womb, birth, parental attention – and inattention – the complex but quite precise Me: it is this that reacts to the large or small range of situations that confronts me. If the range of situations is large, and if the range of my reactions is large too, I may never notice the law that I impose on myself. But it is still there.

The situation, especially people around, may have little effect on my freedom, if they are weak, or if the hold my law has on me is strong. They will not enhance my freedom; but at least they will not curtail it. But circumstances may shatter me, a man may come who can break my law – and impose his. He may increase the range of possibilities open to me; he may narrow it. And even if he increases it, I may not *feel* freer. I may only feel that I have lost the freedom to be bound by the tight little circle of my past where at least I am at home with myself.

What I want is to be made more and more open to a fuller and fuller range of encounter, appreciation, experience, where it is I, but a constantly renewed I, that is giving and receiving. There must be more and more offered and demanded, and *I* must be able to respond and accept. If I am to be free this way, there must be someone so strong that he can break my law's tight hold on me, so powerful that he can always make all things new for me, so attractive and so tender that I am never able to escape into my own protective custody, and never allowed to drag my feet long enough to feel as fetters the bands of his love.

Such a one – real or imaginary – would have to be a man (or a woman), a human figure, a human group. Bone of my bone, flesh of my flesh. He, she, they must live the greater freedom to which I am invited, in the captivity in which I find myself. It must be a truly human liberty that is offered me, if it is to touch me at all. Beyond that I cannot make any condition. The sort of freedom would be up to him, her, them: wealth, poverty; western materialism, eastern spirituality.

If I let myself be so attracted, I would be treating my enchanter as a god; I would be surrendering myself the way men have said you only may to one you believe is God. Only one (only a company) that is godlike could offer me the unending growth in love that is in fact the freedom I covet. I can admire many ordinary human freedoms, receive grace from them; but always there is the looming boundary wall, cramping the finest. Only a godlike freedom could escape disappointing my trust. Some freedoms are offered by anti-Christs: such a one as Hitler. Some I would see as pro-Christs: Karl Marx, say; Buddha; Gandhi. They each offer a good vision. But it is still bounded, and even in thought I soon feel cabin'd, cribb'd, confin'd. Only a true Christ, a real God-Man (really himself alive, or really by me imagined) can offer what I ask. (Yet can my imagination (however fed by others) release me from me? Perhaps it can. I can only suppose that a God-Man himself alive would do it better.)

Of course my wistful thinking, my trembling on the edge of falling in love with love, proves nothing, suggests concretely only a thing or two about me: until something happens. This I have already said. And nothing has yet happened to another or to me that could not be put down to vivid – or perfervid – imagination. (Even that has its credit side: it is part of the price of the free gift of this freedom-that-may-be. If the freedom were quite inescapable it would not be the freedom I am looking for.) If men and women do find this freedom, it may suggest that it is worth joining them. But even finding beyond just wishing won't prove that the path is not a dead-end. And anyway, you may not want this sort of freedom at all: however much it may happen, you may well be free to rest unpersuaded.

Is it necessary to scare away the bogy of determinism? It has been thought that advances in scientific knowledge have made a word like 'freedom' useless; certainly useless in any grand sense. The billiard table; take any one moment, the pattern from then is set: complex but set; predictable, unbendable. 'Nor let anyone at this juncture start whispering in our ears the name of Heisenberg', and 'indeterminacy'. The velocity and position of the smallest individual particles/waves cannot both be predicted. But this may not be more than a temporary resting place; and random chance is no more productive of freedom than an iron determinism. Anyway, we are not using 'freedom' in a grand sense. We are talking of ordinary freedoms and their loss. If the pattern of interaction of every atom and molecule and cell were set – and on our scale, probability is high, uncertainty minimal – a man in prison would still in most cases feel and be less free than a man outside. The man outside can be made more free (if the pattern moves in his favour). He is no less, no more pre-determined. That would be nonsense; if everything is totally pre-determined, there can be neither less nor more. But within the pattern, some complex organisms, men, can be freer or less free. If you read this book and accept it, and if in any way it enlarges your life, fair enough, that it would was determined; but you are that much freer than you were. It was – if you like – determined that you should be made freer. Not less (or more) determined. Just less (or more) narrowly determined. As we have said, you are bound by some law. It depends whether you feel it as law or as freedom, captivity or grace.

Freedom for most men is an increase in breadth and variety of life: and being themselves enabled to enjoy and experience again and again a fresh breadth and variety. It does not matter if this comes through an iron determinism, random chance, or divine providence, if come it does. (Though I may trust it further if I can believe it comes from provident love.)

Only if someone did foretell me my every future action in detail, might I lose my sense of freedom. There would be no freshness, nothing new. But he could not. Logically it is impossible. He has not the time to steal all my freedom by spoiling its surprise. If he tells me too much, he simply leaves no time for his telling to come true. He can only predict an episode. If he did, correctly and in detail, it might get me worried. But he cannot do even that. He foresees that I am going to do $x$, $y$, $z$ – without my knowing that I shall. Now, if he tells me, he adds a fresh factor, disproves his own prediction. Perhaps, then, he predicts that I shall be told that I am 'going to do' $x$, $y$, $z$, *and* that I will respond to this further determining factor by doing $a$, $b$, $c$ (or even $xk$, $yk$, $zk$) instead. But if he tells me *this* in advance, he again ruins his own prediction. And so on.

If I am powerless in some catastrophe, a sense of having 'been there before' may increase my feeling of captive helplessness. But if in fact I find I can take effective action, my sense of familiarity with the surrounding circumstances may well make me feel supremely free.

It may be determined that the idea of determinism will cramp some men's sense of freedom and enjoyment of life. I am determined that it shall not for me; and am determined to help prevent it for others. If Jesus is God enough, he may share with me the full human freedom that was his as a man.

## (ii) Jesus and freedom for the future

The overriding freedom that Jesus has seemed to offer is an openness to 'the future' as a grand whole. He suggests (at least 'suggests': the question of whether the suggestion is usable and, further, likely to be successful, must rest; in what follows there will only be occasional reminders) a critical optimism. This is important. Human beings have a (very necessary) protective device which allows them to close their minds to unpleasant facts and possibilities. If something very terrible is very likely to happen some time soon, and nothing can be done about it, only by forgetting it (or by sickly joking over it) am I at all likely to be able to continue functioning at all, even in the reduced circle left to me. But this means that I can *only* act unrealistically; I can only do what is more or less inappropriate. I may even use this device too soon, and miss a genuine possibility of averting disaster.

Most of us can only face a difficult or threatening future realistically if we are presented with some possibility of dealing with it that convinces us. If you are convinced that the future belongs to the God whose Christ is Jesus, then you may be able to face the future, no matter how ugly it appears. You do not need to withdraw from it into alcohol, lysergic acid, Zen, sex, work, art, courageous despair, prayer, or any other fall-out shelter. You can look at it, size it up, get to grips with it, act. (Of course, Jesus' wounded side may be just another dug-out to cower in. But even that is meant as a withdrawal, the better to advance.)

If Jesus talks of the rule of God, he may be re-interpreting it more or less drastically. But at least he is talking about the future; if not, some other term than 'kingdom' would have been needed. He may be talking primarily about me and my immediate future, rather than about the grand overall drama of the universe. But his friends at least were sure to understand him this way, and he may well have meant the final unfolding of God's plan, as well as the freedom that this gives to me in my response to God and neighbour here and now. But he was speaking about the future, and God's control in and of the future; and himself as its focus as he spoke. Was he to be its focus all through? We have said, maybe. Certainly, for his early followers, this was so. Jesus was the exalted Christ, Lord of the world's future. And so the facts of life, the grim facts of life, could be faced: war, death, disease, famine, demonic forces, space and time; in all, the victory could be theirs.[2]

Of course, the dialectic of history, with Marx and Lenin as its prophets, or the progress of evolution, with Charles Darwin, John Dewey and Julian Huxley, may offer alternative models with similar active functions. These each proclaim that final success is all but certain; and so far from letting you sit down and let it come, they spur you to intense activity, to ease its passage, to avert disasters that might delay the day. The day itself is so bright and sure that every disaster can be faced fairly and squarely and overcome: it looks so small in the day's light.

Such a faith is not necessarily indestructible; and it does not necessarily win its way. The fact of the atomic bomb shook the evolutionary faith of H. G. Wells. The facts of human misery can effectively shatter a Christian's trust.

But while it lasts, a Christian's trust in Jesus as God's Christ, the Lord of the future, gives him one form of wide openness to the future of his world, able to accept the facts, because they cannot for the moment outface him.

It is necessary to accept, once more, that Christ *has* been a way of escape, by focusing attention so firmly on the bright distant future that the present and the nearer future are simply ignored. But this seems a misuse of the model he offers (or comprises). Jesus' own teaching is placed firmly in his contemporary society. It is directed towards realtionships between people in the current social structure (not in some idealized future). Conditions of work, commerce, and so on, are sufficiently continuous with inter-personal life, in his view, to contain parabolic hints (rather than allegorical indices) of the true ways of man and God. Food and clothing – as well as care and concern – are part of the stuff of the life he offers. 'Physical' healing and forgiveness belong together. A man is whole when he is restored to God, health, family, and work. (Only it is sometimes a different family and a different work.)

But more than that (which has to be gleaned; and which is, we have shown, not as comprehensive as some would like), Jesus offers a freedom in this world in a deeper and wider way than is merely suggested by these details.

He acts and talks as one who is at home, precisely in the physical world around him. Not at home, in the sense of in his own unalterable cell, asleep. But at home, in the sense that this is a place that can be altered, decorated, adapted, for human living. He is free to make this place his own, mould it to a shape that fits him. It is his father's house. It is capable of being shaped by his father through him for his father and for him. At least, we have suggested, this is how many of his parables suggest you see and treat your world. This is how he saw it and behaved in it and towards it.

If you read David Jenkins's Bampton Lectures, you will find that he gives great emphasis to this factor, and shows how precisely this major theme was triumphantly preserved in the first four centuries' discussion of Jesus. To affirm

that Jesus is the Logos . . . is to affirm that Jesus is the key to the understanding of the Cosmos, of the realm of things, as well as to the understanding of history, the realm of persons, and that further, and most importantly, the understanding of these two realms must be united.

It is in this world that personal life can flourish, freely, without being destroyed by it, and without withdrawing from it.

Christianity offered a 'new optimism'. It differed from 'the Greek fashion of thinking which optimistically assumed the universe was rational'; and even more from 'the Gnostic fashion of thinking which pessimistically assumed that men and the world did not fit together'.

The Gnostics insisted on, or assumed a complete dualism between the truly spiritual and human, and the givenness of material things and of the events of history. . . . Even Greek optimism had not conceived that man and the Cosmos fitted together in a way that took account of the material and bodily side of man, still less that took account of the serial events of history. It was the purely spiritual, rational and mind side of man which was related to the underlying spiritual and rational pattern of the Universe and which was capable of ignoring the meaningless recurrence of the events of history and of penetrating the mere appearances of material things and so reaching the reality of true and absolute Being.

But, for the Christian, *man and the universe tie together because of the involvement of God to that end*.[3]

The Council of Chalcedon in A.D. 451 'defined' Christian belief in Jesus. He was 'one person in two natures'. ('Person' and 'nature' are technical and *not* self-explanatory translations of Greek technical terms.) In him, all that it means to be truly God is truly God and all that it means to be truly man is truly man, *and* he is one. This is at least a parable, a symbol, a model for a refusal to split man in or from his world.

The questions remain: is it possible to maintain this refusal to split man in or from his world on the basis of other models? (is this model essential as a model?); and, even if it is, is it 'only' a (*the*) model – or can it function as the model for this refusal only because it corresponds to the reality of Jesus and God? (and further again, if this be so, can it only function when it is *believed* to be so? or can it work for someone who does not believe in God – or Jesus – as real?) To put this more simply, is the non-Christian likely to fail to maintain his and others' personalness? are the Christian atheist and Christian historical sceptic likely to fail too? David Jenkins seems to suggest they are. I am (as I have said) by no means sure that this is so.

Whatever the answers you give to these questions, David Jenkins has certainly shown that the classical debates about Jesus are at least in part also debates about man and his world. And the outcome of these debates includes an insistence that man can live fully in the 'material' and 'serial' world that he is part of. To return to our terms 'freedom' and 'openness', a Christian should find himself free and open to the future precisely in the physical world of cause and effect. This is at the heart of the Christ-model, the freedom that Jesus lived and that the Spirit offers.

## (iii) Jesus and freedom from the past

Freedom for the future involves necessarily freedom from the past; and that, as we have seen, has to include my past. And Jesus is presented in the gospels as one who conveys forgiveness, sets a man free from the guilt, failure (and disease) that bind and cripple him. Forgiveness can seem, for this reason, a very negative term (and Paul, for instance, does not use it much). It can appear to be merely a scouring, a cleansing. This is not presented as Jesus' intention: for instance, the parable of the room 'swept and garnished' makes the inadequacy of this approach quite plain. Freedom from the past is on its own valueless, unless at the same time you are given a real freedom for the future. (Remember, we are looking for the moment primarily at what is offered in Jesus as God's Christ. We are leaving to the next and last chapter the question of whether the offer can be fulfilled, and how.)

The offer has often been presented as 'be sorry, and you'll be forgiven'. This is a misinterpretation (suggested by a few passages in Acts, only). Jesus is presented as able to free you from your past at a stage much earlier than your beginning to feel sorry about it, much earlier than any sense of failure. He accepts a man (or a woman) as friend, or friend and follower; and if the man or woman accepts Jesus' acceptance (God's acceptance in Jesus), then there is the break from the past and the new openness to the future. But the break begins in Jesus' act; sorrow, penitence, remorse (if there is time for these luxuries) have to wait – certainly, in most cases. 'Repent!' can only mean something like, 'Let the offer of the rule of God turn your attention – and intentions – in this totally new direction.'

Paul, we have noted, does not much use the term 'forgiveness'. He prefers the complicated legal term usually translated 'justify', but perhaps better, 'set right'. (Against its Old Testament background, it almost certainly means more than just 'acquit'.) But more meaningful for us is a less frequent term of Paul's (but one he uses in a similar way): 'accept'. God in Christ has accepted us. This means that the past hold of 'sin' is broken, and a man is free for God and his neighbour in this world. Again, the first act is God's, and our response – faith, trust – follows. God's act is first in the death and resurrection to glory of Jesus; and in the offer of acceptance to each individual, and in the invitation to trust. (But, of course, tautologically, the acceptance only becomes 'real' for the individual when the individual accepts it as real for him, when he believes. And so the complete reality of acceptance depends on faith: but starts from God.)

There is a more elaborate 'mythological' picture in Paul. He can speak of the freedom that is offered in terms of freedom from angelic or demonic 'powers'. These are the factors that have bound a man in his past. They are, at least in part, what we might term economic, political, social, intellectual 'forces' (it is not a straight equivalence; but there is an appreciable overlap). They are *not* just totally abolished. A man remains in a world where they still operate: this world. But he is not dominated by them: they (and the world they represent) are the area where he exercises his new liberty. In terms of the myth-picture, Christ has triumphed over them.[4]

(It is worth noticing that Paul too accepts that 'freedom' is relative. There is a sense in which the non-Christian has freedom: freedom from Christ. And the Christian, in turn, gains one freedom at the expense of another: he is free from, but not free for, the old gods; he is free for, because slave of, Christ.)[5]

If you have come across any discussion of 'the Atonement', of what God was up to in the case of Jesus, you may well have found some of the ideas bizarre, and some even downright unpleasant. God tricks the devil into losing his rightful claim to us, the devil's captives, by letting him lay claim to Jesus, to whom he could have no right. Or, Jesus seized us from the devil as helpless prisoners, by brute 'spiritual' force. Or, God's honour had been slighted by our sin, but was restored when the one innocent victim was foully done to death. Or, God's anger was assuaged when he was allowed to wreak his vengeance on this sinless man. Or, God's justice was satisfied when this man was unjustly executed. And so on. As symbols for what God might be up to, or as models for life in this world, these are totally inadequate. But as pictures evoking an enormous sense of relief, or freedom, they are very expressive. They say, You can be like a man relieved of an impossible fine, substituted for in front of a firing squad, bailed out at the cost of a friend's life. You can be a man set free from the shackles of your past.

The other type of 'Atonement theory' is often technically termed 'moral influence', and fastened on Peter Abélard. A 'moral influence' theory expresses the possibility of openness for the future. Christ is our pattern and example, and as such moves us to a loving response. The failure of this approach on its own has lain in its inability to treat with the need for freedom from the past (especially my own), that holds me unmoved. Both pictures belong together; but Pauline terms like 'acceptance', 'justification', 'reconciliation', express the two aspects in one whole, and avoid the uneasy tension that occurs in later discussion.

## (iv) Jesus and freedom from law

For Paul, the freedom offered in Christ includes freedom from 'law'. This is not freedom from all law (we have suggested that this is impossible; Paul comes to the same conclusion, though not necessarily by the same route). It is freedom from any model for life that binds my future wholly or even in part to my past, to 'success' or 'failure' in my past. Law is still there, but it is not a 'law of works'. And, equally, my further future is not bound by my 'success' or 'failure' in my immediate future. This is the essential freedom for acceptance for which Paul fights. Many of his Jewish-Christian contemporaries seem to have been able to live this freedom within the framework of the Jewish law (and Paul clearly allows for this possibility. The grand Psalm 119 celebrates another freedom of this sort). But Paul himself finds that to live his new freedom in any one given pattern risks losing it for himself, and prevents his sharing it with others. For a while, (even a long while), a given framework may protect me from being bound by my own narrower past. But for Paul, it seemed fatally easy to slip back into being determined by my success or failure in this framework, into being closed off by it from my new neighbours.

It is impossible to abolish all law; but *any* given law is put severely in question by the freedom that is offered in

God's acceptance of us in Christ. To accept the crucified Jesus as God's Christ, as your model for life, is to undermine all your moral decency, all your allegiance to respected conventions.

For instance, it has long been held in religious circles in Europe and America that your freedom for (marriage to) a particular person depends heavily on your freedom from previous coition with another, and still more on your freedom from prior contracts. Jesus has seemed to reinforce this, and even complicate the matter further with questions of lustful inclinations. None the less, he and Paul made all this very insecure, as 'law' (so that it becomes, instead, good advice). Taken as a legal pronouncement, it cannot logically be part of a model that includes their thought and practice. For they offer a model (or models) in which no failure, and no success, in the past can guarantee your freedom or your captivity in the future. They say (we still defer consideration of whether it is more than words) that whatever your past, you can be made free by God through Christ, for God and your neighbour in the future.

Of course, present freedoms can exclude each other. You cannot make love to two people at the same time; you cannot give your complete attention to each of two competing people at the same moment. And what you do now may have a very great effect on your future freedom: it may make it easier or harder to be open to the next encounter. Paul (in Romans 7) on most people's interpretation certainly found this. And if this incident loses you a limb, or a lobe of your brain, you will not be free to grow it again for the next. Allowing these qualifications (which can savagely destroy any freedom) you are offered in Jesus always a full fresh freedom for love. There need be no mental, psychological barrier of guilt, sense of failure, fear, emotional withdrawal between you and God and your neighbour.

I say this is a full freedom. It could, of course, be very shallow. A constant erasure of the past would void any present relationship or activity of almost all content. It would be so childlike as to be positively senile: never remembering or never referring to what was done or said a moment back. There is no hint that this is what is offered. The Paul who lives a new life in Christ is the Paul who always remembers that he persecuted the Church; remembers, too, that his Pharisaism was completely satisfying while it lasted. The past is remembered, and is part of the present relationship: but it does not decide what present part it is to play, and it is not the dominant factor. (The past may be better remembered for this reason.) You are free to let a new exchange of love and caring develop, so that all your past leads into it, and there is no petrified stubborn block of thought, deed, saying that will be able to resist for long the new movement. Your past is neither a prison nor a fortress, to hold you captive or to repulse others (not even a place from which you must escape, and to which you dare not return). The whole of your past can become flexible, malleable, adaptable; stuff from which each new activity, each new relationship can draw substance.

This freedom, then, offers to deepen and enrich your living. Because you are free from the past, you are free for the past. Because you are accepted in full knowledge of your past, you are not chained to it in glad, angry, contented or sad subservience, and you are able yourself to accept your own past. This is the freedom of Jesus the man, offered to you (I trust) by Jesus who is God. It is a freedom you cannot win; only hope to be given, and be enabled to receive.

# (v) Jesus and freedom for others

That you are accepted and so are able to accept yourself means that you are able to accept others. (Remember, I have undertaken not to discuss yet whether or how this happens. I am here outlining formally a Christian 'style of life', the life that is accepted when you accept Jesus as God's Christ; as the second person of the undivided Trinity; as a model for life in this world: or however you phrase it. I am not here attempting to point to it in action.) You are able to accept others, as they are, because nothing in their past need form a block. Of course, they may refuse your acceptance. But if you do take the initiative, the fact of your acceptance, the potential in what you offer, or something, may create the situation in which the hard frozen blocks in the other begin to soften and melt, so that they will slip more or less easily into the new relationship that is being created, the new shared activity that is being undertaken.

In Christ, says Paul (or a pupil), there is neither Jew nor Greek, bond nor free, male nor female. That does not mean that everyone turns into an androgynous, cultureless, stereotyped lump. The Jew becomes a Christian Jew, the Hellene a Christian Hellene, the barbarian a Christian barbarian. (Of course, our impression of the nineteenth century is of attempts to turn Polynesians into Christian Victorian petty-bourgeois: we are examining the ideals, not at present the failures.) It is possible, then, to accept the other as he is (if he will), without his first becoming a Christian of some sort, still less of your or my sort. This must be; because only on the basis of a prior acceptance can he in this sense become a Christian at all, however much he wills it.[6]

I can accept him, be accepted by him, without having

109

first, or soon afterwards, to change him, convert him (though change will come, to him and to me). I may find Christ in him as he is (if I will) without feeling that I need first to put Christ in him – and so may more truly find him. (I do not, though, have to say it this way.) Ideally, this creates a freedom to talk about the things that matter most to each one, a freedom to engage together in activities, even, where there is theoretical disagreement between us.

If you do enjoy a freedom like this, overt intolerance is obviously impossible. But so, too, should be the insult of patronizing tolerant curiosity, where the other becomes a casual anthropological specimen, New Zealander, Nigerian, North American, South Briton, East-Ender. Instead, the other's facts, feats, and fancies are worth a passionate involvement, for or against, on the basis of your firm acceptance of him. You are free to take him or her really seriously. You have at least the possibility of a constructive disagreement. It is an extremely important freedom in a time of great mobility.

It is extremely important in the context of any current Marxist-socialist society. Elisabeth Adler's book, 'Pro-Existence', is a fine example. Here there are Christians who oppose strongly the dogmatic atheist materialism in Marxism, but are able to disagree constructively. If this (Christian) freedom were more widely shared, it would offer at least *an* answer to threats of war and the apparent need for suicidal deterrents. Of course it is difficult, and you risk finding the other closed into an impenetrable shell of wickedness: Nazism and Munich and Neville Chamberlain's very Christian attempt to disagree constructively. It is impossible just to seize this freedom in the absence of the others that should go with it. Your acceptance of the other into this sort of relationship will hardly ever create an immediate response. If your dealings with him up till then have been quite different (and if your new tolerance is based on fear) then you may well suffer a massive rebuff. The situation that the great powers, including Britain, had created in Germany between the wars was not one in which a sudden generous acceptance (however genuine) was likely to be itself acceptable and creative. But this only suggests that a policy of mutual rejection is very likely to be destructive; a more open attitude at least contains the possibility of a positive outcome. (Can nations whose individual citizens do not exercise a Christian freedom exercise it for them? We can at least suggest that it might be worth their leaders' trying.)[7]

If the richer nations were willing to 'waste' their resources on giving technical skills (industry, medicine, population control), loans, guaranteed prices, along with a personal and cultural interchange on a large scale, a context for a genuine freedom might emerge. Certainly the Christians at least among their leaders should find this worth the risk.[8]

Back to the individual scene: for the Christian, a risk like this in his own life is always worth the taking. The freedom he has received is a costly one, it always includes a risk; the possibility or the presence of suffering. The model has at its heart one who was free enough for the people he accepted to risk death at their hands. A Christian's freedom to accept others has to include this passivity, this permission to the other to take even a cruel initiative. This is the measure of the breadth and depth of the openness involved. (Whether a nation could take on itself this openness and risk has still to be seen. To date, there seem to be only instances of individuals and small groups – the Derbyshire village that lived with the plague; and only recommendations from groups and individuals – Jeremiah and unilateral disarmers – to nations for nations to ignore.)

There are many other arenas for a Christ-styled freedom. There is the risk involved in sitting lightly to wealth and security within any given pattern of society. This is an essential part of Christian freedom. You do not foreclose the future for the sake of maintaining the mortgage on your house. Perhaps hardest of all for many is the possession of comparative wealth (in this country, even a pensioner is wealthy) and its generous use. (It is easier just to refuse it, or to get completely rid of it.)

And Christian freedom includes an intellectual freedom that involves the freedom to enquire into and to doubt the very basis and structure of that faith and freedom itself; and enfolds every preceding diverse possibility. A Christian *par excellence* should be open to every idea that another man has seriously held or lightly enjoyed. There are physical limits (mental-physical). There are no logical limits to a Christian's freedom of enquiry. He is free, supremely free, to roam as far as his mental and physical condition allow in the material and serial and intellectual universe around him.

He is bound by no Luddite fear of robots and computers and test-tube reproductions of foetal development. He looks forward to a future with minimal work and maximum leisure. In all this he expects to find an increase in depth and richness of personalness, caring, love.

To accept Jesus as Christ, Lord, Son of God, Son of Man, Prophet, model for life, is to accept the dangerous gift of this freedom (to refuse this freedom is then to refuse him as all or any of these). To accept this freedom as a gift from him – as a man who died, as God who rose, or as a constructed but compelling model for living, is to accept him as Lord in a sense that has certainly a lot in common with that in the New Testament writers: Lord of life, Lord of the Universe, Lord of the forces of the natural and human-natural world, Lord of the future.

Not everyone who says, Lord, Lord, . . .
Not everyone who says, the second person of the holy and
undivided Trinity, consubstantial, co-eternal, . . .
Not everyone who says, this is the man for me, . . .
But he who does the will of my father in heaven . . .
Shall enter the kingdom,
Shall find he has accepted his acceptance,
Shall exercise and enjoy the freedom.
But that becomes tautology, true by definition only.
Can it really happen – and how? and where?

# 7. The Man for Us and the God for Us

## (i) How?

BOOKS can only do what books are good for. They can convey information, make suggestions, arouse feelings, let logic be unfolded; but they are in themselves very unpractical. You can prop up chair legs or line rooms with them; but there are usually better materials to hand. And a book may be very content to have no further consequence, or no further traceable consequence (other than that you buy the author's or the publisher's next). But this is a book that suggests that you should receive a gift. It trusts that it is a real gift. But it cannot prove that the gift is real, or offered to you. The most it can do is persuade you to try, persuade you that the risk is worth taking.

It may be that already for a lifetime you have been enjoying what this book is trying haltingly to point to – enjoying the freedom of the service of the man Jesus as God. And if you have been enjoying it, you will have been trying to share it. It could even be that, reading this book, or one of the others I have suggested, you found you were open to the power of the servant Lord, and his freedom is yours, and the words make sense. But that too will have torn you open or soothed you open – or both – to more and more people around you; it has done, or it will. Because that is the sort of freedom he offers, an openness to new friends to serve (by giving or by receiving) and to serve with.

And this may all be so to a much greater degree than it is for me, the writer. I do myself find something of this freedom in words and books (and pictures and buildings and music). But above all I find it among people. I may in fact take it to them in some measure. And it is never quite unrelated to the words of Jesus and the words about the Christ. But it is with another person, with other people, from them, that I receive this freedom in a way that gives meaning to his words and to other's words and to my own. And they do not even need to be aware of him (though that helps) and they do not need to use the same words. But other people are an essential part of this freedom, part of its essence and structure. There are other freedoms – including ones that people have enjoyed in Jesus' name. But his freedom is a freedom to be loved by, and to love, people.

The dawning of this openness may come apart from other people, or even in spite of them. But it cannot – logically cannot – grow and strengthen apart from them. It is at its very heart bound up with them.

If you look at Christian life as the following of a pattern of behaviour (and I have used this way of talking) then it makes good enough sense to try to share this with other people. Some people solve some problems best in groups. A friend, a small group, a crowd, may encourage different individuals – and groups – at different times to different things. Guy Fawkes and Captain Scott and Al Capone and Francis of Assisi need fellow conspirators, explorers, gangsters, believers; David needs Jonathan, Holmes needs Watson; the England team need the England crowd, Billy Graham needs the Harringay crowd, a lyncher needs his mob; MRA needs its groups, Communism its cells. Quite a lot of work has been done and more is in progress on 'group dynamics', the way groups work, and their effects on individuals and the outcome in the group itself. Crowd study is more difficult. Two- and three-person relationships have been analysed for longer. But everyone knows that a lot of people – not all; or not all at every point – work better or follow their hobbies with greater enthusiasm in the company of others.[1]

But the other and the others are more deeply necessary to Christian life than they are to, say, stamp-collecting or psychotherapy or hymn-singing or riots. An individualist may be a good man on his own; but even he cannot belong to Christ on his own. His fellow men may fray his sort of goodness. But if he is to live a Christian goodness, his fellow men are essential to the venture, and he may just have to put up with losing his goodness if he is to be free to love instead.

This was Jesus' freedom, and he received it and offered it and secured its acceptance as one of a small circle of friends. Being an ordinary man, he needed these others for their encouragement and to gain insight from their insight and from their blindness. A present-day sociologist would have been able to recognize and then very likely predict the pattern of relationships and actions in this group: even the defection of Judas and the denial by Peter. But this group was a necessary part of Jesus' freedom for men and for God at a much deeper level – just because it was this sort of freedom he enjoyed and offered.

116

The group of friends and followers is not an accident. It is not a convenience for protection or propaganda or insurance against loss of the message; not even a means of transmitting the gift (though this last is important). The gaggle of friends who understand so little is at the same time part of the life and freedom and openness itself, a part of the power of God. The word of God's love takes flesh not in a solitary hero but in an ordinary man who is part of a rather nondescript group of men. Because this is the sort of love it is. There was no other way. The human life that God made his own, and the freedom for God and men which made up that life were bound up with the coming to freedom of a dozen or so others. They are bound so closely that they are part of the same event, essential in the saving of the world by God's love for God's love.

If you put this in terms of 'the Church', it may well mislead. 'The Church' looks so much like (at best) a means to an end that does not – you hope cannot – include it; skiers encouraging each other on their individual paths; a corporation for the continued repetition of a message or a story or a ballet; a society for preserving ancient monuments – or for the maintenance pure and simple of itself – or the political and social and economic importance of its leading members. A signpost to God who is somewhere else. Maybe this Church, these Churches, have little to do with the matter at all. Or they do these other jobs and point to a reality that happens elsewhere and almost in spite of them; and then sometimes right in the sorriest parts of them; and even where the institution looks healthy and strong.[2]

Jesus lived his freedom for others with others for whom he was free, and deeply free. His invitation to love was promiscuous; but at its heart and centre was a faithful commitment to the group that was there first and foremost for the living and wider sharing of this freedom, and for no other important reason.

And Paul and John and Luke and the others tell us that this is how they found that Jesus' freedom could still be theirs after his death. If the context was there, the freedom could happen. It could happen even more than it did when Jesus was there. 'The Church is the Body of Christ.' 'This is how we know that he abides in us: we know it when we love one another.'

It is in a group, a cell, a small society, which focuses itself on Jesus as the gift of God's love to us, that you can expect to receive and share and grow in Jesus' freedom; and because it is a freedom for others, you can expect to share it and receive it more and more widely.

If this does happen for you or another, then this book has some truth in it. There is no other persuasion.

If this does happen for you or another, it is only persuasion. There is no proof that the freedom you find real is the gift of real God. Though if it is this freedom, it must be a gift, albeit someone else's. The uncommitted man is of course still free to say, 'Well, I always knew a group could have strong effects on its members – even crazier things than this could happen.' But the group would want to say otherwise – at least to itself.

This love sees itself as a gift. The individual joining the group and receiving the gift can readily say, 'It is their gift to me. Not I, but the love of these people having its effect on me. Not a freedom I wrest for myself, but a freedom that grows on me in this company.'

It is not so easy for the group, when it has come to be an entity, an organic whole that can see itself as one in relation to other groups and individuals and things around.

It can say, 'Not us, but the grace of this man Jesus, as we

read the record of men's responses to him.' And this may very well work, and allow the pattern of the love and freedom and service to increase in its proper depth and complexity. But the group will know that others focus their attention here, and little or nothing happens. Others express a trust in Jesus as God or the gift of God, and remain narrowly bound and restricted in old ways along well-trodden paths. 'Why us? Is it perhaps some power in us, some inner dynamic, something that we as a group – or as individuals – generate?'

And an early Christian answer is, 'No, not the group, but the Spirit of God empowering us'. Not the *esprit de corps*, but the Holy Ghost. I have already suggested the importance of this term (and other books in this series will deal with it more fully; and also with 'the Church' in its time of renewed 'Reformation'). It is a traditional term; it has had a wide (and, of course, very varied) use. New Testament writers could as well talk of the power of God, the wisdom of God, the rule of God. The term has often worked well. It is worth trying it in this part of the pattern. It fits well when we are concentrating on freedom and love: at least, these are its strongest overtones in Pauline writing. 'The love of God is poured into our hearts by the Holy Spirit which he gave us.' 'Where the Spirit of the Lord is, there is liberty.'

It is at least arguable that where a group expects to be fired by 'the Spirit', 'God in action', and directs its gratitude here, its experience of growth in freedom and new freedoms will be richer. At least, the term fits. Past and present, larger groups who claim the Spirit have been much more open to newness and variety and change and so freedom. Nor is the disturbance (it does not have to be) purely arbitrary. It is the Spirit of Jesus or the Spirit of the God of Jesus. But it is Spirit, power, disturbance, action.[3]

It is a term that has served well. It has helped men to expect great things. There have been long periods when it has been little used – and then only in formal settings, such as the ordination of ministers in the institution. These have been times when freedom and love have been cramped and weakened. But the words alone have little importance. It is a simple question: Do they or do they not help in the living of this life? If it can be lived without them, then well and very good.

Where some group finds the freedom to love this way, a love which is always a gift to individual and to group, then the life and love and freedom of Jesus are real again. There he is risen Lord and Christ. There he is the man for us and the God for us. The Spirit is given. There, there is real human life that points to (though it can never prove) the life of God who is love.

## (ii) Where?

The freedom for others of the man Jesus may come to you when you have very little contact with the life of any group that claims him. This seems to have happened, though very rarely. But I have suggested that if it is an authentic version of Jesus' freedom it will drive you into a growing network of growing relationships. Here it will find fresh substance and growth and scope. But it leaves you with the question, Where is such a structure to be found?[4]

It genuinely may be enough to look for a building with a stone cross on it, and join in something that happens there on Sunday. The Mass, the Parish Communion, the Service of the Breaking of the Word, vigorous hymns, languorous Evensong, or a liturgically solemn Quaker silence: all these are set to preserve in some way, and offer, the memory of Jesus' freedom and the way in which that memory was shared in early days (and in more recent times).

It is possible through these formal ways to find a deepening and enriching of Christian love. You are then driven into relationships with other people, Christian or not, in which what has been pointed to happens, now perhaps without any explicit reference to Christ. In worship alongside fellow Christians you are laid open to quite other people in other places, to love and be loved by. And if this happens, it is surely very good.

Much the same result may come from listening to the radio, listening to and watching television, when some act of worship is being relayed. Music, theatre, ballet, films, painting – from Christian or non-Christian sources – may offer the point where this freedom begins or is renewed, re-directed, enlightened. The test whether this is merely a religious form of self-indulgence comes afterwards, when you examine the sort of difference, if any, that is made in your relation to other people.

Ecclesiastical machines cannot (any more than this or another book or a play) guarantee to re-create in any applicant the freedom and love that are the life of Christ. They maintain well-tested conditions in which it is known that this life can happen. The conditions, the 'means' of grace (in varying forms) are there. It may not even be all that difficult to predict which people will be most success-fully seized and liberated, by which means of grace. But in none is success automatic for every applicant.

The Churches are deceptive institutions. They may deliberately or by default give the impression that just the maintenance of the conditions, the means of grace, is the living of the Christ-life. But Christ is not real just because the ceremony or the silence are repeated.

And perhaps the least lively results can come from trying to force the issue, trying to ensure that people are affected at least in some way by what goes on, emotionally stirred, or 'edified', or something. But because the freedom we look for is always a freedom for others, I can almost – *almost* – guarantee failure if my first question is 'What effect did (or will) that have on me?' Jesus' openness to others was grounded in his openness to God. If the means of grace is worship, if it is an activity that claims to point to God, then it must do that. On the basis of the offering of the mass or the music or the meditation to God, forgetful of ourselves, we may be in fact caught into the offering, laid open to him who is love, and so to the others he loves.

The same must apply for other means of grace – art, theatre, music. If they engage me first and foremost with myself – or if I demand that they do – then it is a restricted sort of grace I shall most likely (not certainly) receive. For sure, they must engage me; but they must point me in compassion and acceptance and understanding and delight to people around to love and be loved. (I cannot write more about these 'secular' means of grace. They play, I think, a subsidiary part for me. If they seem more promising to you, I can only offer you my encouragement, and some other authors that you may find helpful.)[5]

These 'means of grace', pointers and stimulants to Christ's freedom and love, will have worked only when they have brought you into a full contact with other people around. They are not themselves grace. The grace, the life, the freedom for others can only be where these others are, whoever they are. If Church, liturgy, activity, group, art or science keeps you from them they are not means of grace but barriers to it, chains to be thrown off and destroyed.

The most 'natural' place to look for the living of Jesus' style of life, open and free for others, is in marriage. For many people, the other's free gift of herself, himself to me, on trust, saying there are no reservations, makes the first point where 'love' in a Christian sense is glimpsed. Compared with that, the best that went before is a mere altruistic hedonism. And the glimpse of love is firmed and drawn out in the gift of life to new beings, babies, helpless tyrants, innocent egotists.

Even this is obviously corruptible, and, even at its best, corrupting. Sexual play is so appealing and rewarding; and it is so easy to mould your family, partner included, into an extension of yourself which permits a guiltless selfishness that can be terrible. The family becomes a unit, a person to the world, dominated by one, or dominating all its members. But here, because the means of grace is bound up from the start with persons, it can be more than the means, the pointer; it can itself be the place where grace happens, and freedom and openness are created. In this case the family itself becomes directed outward, and is able to accept fresh people into itself; and directs its own members out into wider relations and sustains them there until in one sense it dies, as new groupings – work, service, play, marriage – are formed. Its ability to die (and be reborn) as children leave home is a test of its Christ-likeness. The rebirth is in the increasing range of life of the parent couple.[6]

The formal, traditional 'means of grace' stand in some contrast. They so often seem to be designed and offered for large numbers to share in at once. The ritual activities, sounds, or silence take place in buildings that hold three hundred or a thousand or more in one 'room'. These have often, in the past, in times of strength at least, been balanced by meetings of Christians in much smaller numbers. The Methodist class-meeting has balanced the Central Hall; the extended family (three or more generations, aunts and uncles, domestic servants) has gathered for prayer and Bible reading; the Sunday School has had classes for all ages; the large parish church has had a college of eight priests; the great monastery an establishment of maybe no more than twenty.

When the public ritual has continued with only large numbers who are never more than audience, 'hearing Mass' or 'hearing the Word', it has risked losing its real point. It may still work, but there is less in the structure to help it work, and check whether or not it has any real effect. Some may find the true grace of God here; but others may be shielded from him by it; and others left feeling that there is only a mass impersonal façade of activity, with nothing behind it at all, nothing where they may be drawn in and set free.

Recently I heard tell of an attack by a Catholic student of worship on 'mammoth congregations': and that meant anything over twelve people. The ritual acts, the Eucharist, Mass, Lord's Supper or Holy Communion, may happen better in a room with eight or ten people taking part. They can talk before and after about the world or the words in the liturgy or both. In the parish I serve at present we construct together this way the next Sunday's sermon for the larger gathering. But this is at the same time a 'breaking of the word' for ourselves, in which the freedom and love of Christ come more real for us. It is not automatic. It is sometimes hard to let ourselves go, to admit that we do not see things. It can be even harder to admit that we do see, and the struggle *not* to act on what we see is fierce.

Maybe a greater freedom for God, a greater sharing in the Christ-life in the whole world around can come if the means of grace is a group, a cell talking over some problem of local or national or international concern, with a wider membership than at present can or will share the Eucharist.

124

Christian insights emerge, as Christians and others grapple with situations in which they are committed to action. (They do not need to be sad or destructive problems – though they may be. They may be questions of how best to use some gift, some amenity; how best to share an art exhibition, concert, park, garden, river, social centre.) The group may eat and drink together, go to theatres, watch television. It may meet weekly, once a month, three or four times a year. It will discover, if only for a while, a pattern in which the group and the members find themselves more open to each other, and to people in the world around, and to the world around as a whole.

I would expect any reformation of the life of Churches to centre in the creation and maintenance of small groups and cells of this sort, gathered in common concern for others, and so finding the freedom of Christ. The Churches would stop trying to lord it over the neighbourhood by having the largest building, or at least the largest and oldest and most solemn auditorium. They would take on a much more reticent air, giving in real freedom a genuinely humble service. The institutions would stop claiming rights to pride and self-preservation that they seem now to pretend are wrong only in individuals: a social ethic applied to the Churches themselves. Their pattern of life would then look to members and strangers more like the style of the servant Lord they claim.[7]

But it would surprise me if non-Christian groups, committees, boards never found anything of this freedom in common concern for others. The meeting of psychiatrists and social workers; therapeutic groups as such; co-ordination councils for welfare workers; committees of councils and of parliament; ward party meetings; local or area wives' groups; trade union meetings; even board meetings. The results are often far from 'godless' or 'graceless'. Certainly I would expect God to act where men and women were trying to be open among themselves in concern for others.

And where the house church, the trustees' meeting, the clergy staff council, the chapter, the conference have people who are using them, jockeying for position, solving just their own problems at anyone's expense; then I would expect God to be hampered, and little of the life of Christ to recur. But I would expect meetings of boards of directors to start off with great initial disadvantages: there are such individual and sectional interests at stake. But not even free enterprise capitalism is totally corrupt; just as monastic chapters are not impregnably holy.

Where individuals as persons are trying to be concerned together for others as persons, I would expect something of the character of the life of Jesus to be reproduced. The members may or may not be interested in Jesus as such, may or may not trust him as a living figure. They may differ on this. But if something of his style of life does emerge, then that is as near to resurrection and the life of the Spirit as I would hope for the present to find. That points for me, for some of us, at any rate, to the Jesus whose life is being received, shared, continued, made real again. At least in a 'poetic', metaphorical sense, Jesus is alive again in what happens. Christians have wanted to believe him more than metaphorically alive. If his style of life can be re-lived, then it is at any rate a live metaphor. If these things do not happen, then it is not even a live question.

A group, a cell, a team, that finds this sort of freedom in concern for others may be one that meets as part of its members' paid work. It could be made up of people who live near; of workers in a factory or office; patrons of some café, restaurant, or pub; travellers on a bus or train; friends who never see each other between cell meetings. There is nothing set; except that numbers will rarely exceed a dozen.

The pattern of meeting may be extremely informal. A group will happen because several people decide together that they want it. Or it may have a more formal structure, affiliated with perhaps a national or even international organization, 'secular' or ecclesiastical.

It may be formed to support the work of Oxfam or the United Nations Organization or the International Red Cross. It may be a residents' association, or the committee of a ward political party; a repertory theatre patrons' club, or a wild-life preservation trust. A few adults may be learning a foreign language in evening classes; some neighbours may find they have been independently visiting the elderly in their homes, and decide to meet to co-ordinate and ensure continuity. A handful of doctors or plumbers or journalists or electricians or teachers may set about examining critically their professional standards – or technical competence – or something quite unrelated.

You probably belong already to one or a number of groups of the sort I have listed; you may know very much more than I do of their Christian possibilities. Or what I say may ring a bell, offer you something to hope for, something to recognize and react to if it happens, to recognize and take the chance to share the life and freedom of Christ.

Then again, nothing of this sort may offer. If what I say makes any sense, you may want to know where you can find some cell, some group where Christian freedom is lived more explicitly, so that you can write to a central office for an address, hopefully.

## (iii) Some names

I can only list some books. First, there is one edited by Peter Smith (and published in 1964 by the then firm of

Peter Smith), a five-shilling 140-page paperback called *The Caring Church*. In it a number of writers give a short account of the life and work of various active Christian organizations. The tone is largely Anglican; but many of them have no necessary ecclesiastical ties. In it, Chad Varah talks about 'the Samaritans', people who accept a fair amount of training, go on a rota for manning a telephone that is listed in the directory; and care for anyone who is suicidal, or just in need of human contact or 'non-judgemental' advice. The 'Samaritan' is probably just going to be a friend; but he can be that knowing that he is part of a team that can muster many forms of competent technical advice if it is called for. What is offered (by those who do and those who do not belong to churches) is a compassionate friendship and concern for the other person as a person in their own right; a compassion that is willing to suffer. (Marriage Guidance Counsellors offer a similar concern in their delimited but wide field.)

J. T. Hughes writes of 'Alcoholics Anonymous' (which again has a wider than orthodox Christian membership). People who have been cured of the addiction that has become a disease form a very firm forgiving society that can offer healing even to the seriously crippled.

'The Servants of Christ the King' are a more explicitly religious organization, described here by Olive Parker. Their outward activities vary considerably. Their formal structure offers an interesting and attractive pattern, aimed at giving the most inarticulate a place in deliberations, and allowing room for the most tender or stubborn conscience – it may be both.

There are other movements that were once daring innovations, and are now respectable institutions. The Young Men's and the Young Women's Christian Associations; the men's and women's church meetings (in Anglican terms, the Church of England Men's Society and the Mothers' Union) probably can be as hidebound and introvert as the jokes suggest. But they can also be points where persons can love and be loved and grow wider and deeper in sympathy and concern. Peter Smith's essayists give further instances. There is a list, at the back of this book, of books that tell of the renewal of Christian life in these sorts of ways in other countries: Scotland, France, Germany, and the United States.

A particularly exciting book from the United States is Harvey Cox's recent *The Secular City* (published in U.K. by Student Christian Movement Press Ltd, price one guinea). The style of writing is American, but what he has to say throws a hopeful light on what is happening in many people's lives today. He suggests ways in which modern city life offers us a framework in which there is a real possibility of genuine freedom and responsibility and openness to people as persons and for no other reason. He then points to ways in which in America and elsewhere Christians and others (or others and Christians) have got together to help to make sure that the good is not spoiled or stifled; and to help criticize and fight against the evil and depersonalization that also can result from the same complex technical processes. There is a lot to be done. The making of personal contacts which rest at that level is not enough. It is a matter of being aware of the opportunities, helping other people to be aware; and getting things done, moved, changed. This will often mean (always mean?) direct or indirect political action, protest, agitation. But if each city is driven or cajoled into living up to its promise for all its citizens, it can be a place where a Christian freedom and style of life may be lived and shared.

# (iv) Freedom and the secular

The adjective in Harvey Cox's title, 'secular', and the word 'secularization' crop up quite frequently in Christian discussion these days. Till recently, they have been used to express dismay and still are in some Christian circles. But now there is growing up a much more positive appreciation of what is called 'the process of secularization'. Men are less cramped and bound by religious or irreligious beliefs. They have a much wider range of choice presented to them. They are not so tied to one, maybe inherited, role. They can look more squarely at 'the facts'. For sure they realize more deeply the difficulties involved in isolating 'the facts'; but this is only the other side of being free to choose from among a greatly enlarged range of plausible interpretations.

To choose first an illustration that flatters a westerner: the 'cultural revolution' in China seems (in September 1967) to be a rear-guard action against a genuine 'secularization'. Mao Tse-tung and the Red Guards have been fighting to impose a preconceived pattern (or patterns) of thought on factory managers, farming experts, soldiers, doctors, economists, teachers, who have been attempting to develop skills that will work, irrespective of any orthodoxy. Russian Marxism, by way of contrast, has been slowly giving up its attempts to interfere with scientific autonomy. Notoriously, Christian Churches in the past made determined efforts to censor the results of large areas of research; and this may still be done in establishments under sectarian control.

By way of contrast, there is now being developed an appreciative Christian critique of secularization. It points the extent to which the freedom that it makes possible is paralleled by the freedom which Jesus lived and which his first followers found they could share. They asserted a freedom against any religious pattern that shut them off from other men. They asserted that the world was a place where this sort of freedom really could be lived (even though that also meant a struggle). They refused to allow any 'power' the right to interfere. The historical question as to the indebtedness of modern technology and science to this Christian faith, to Jewish and Christian attitudes, to the Jewish and Christian and Greek heritage, is, I have suggested, uncertain. But whatever the relative importance of these and other factors in producing the present possibility, the present does seem to offer just the sort of freedom to manœuvre that a Christian would wish for. This should be where he could live to the full the gift of the freedom of Jesus his God.[8]

The present does not (as David Jenkins and Abraham Heschel, for instance, point out in passages quoted above) guarantee the desired result. Harvey Cox indicates the very real dangers in the modern city. Marxism is tempted to dogmatize and police on the basis of one stage in sociological and technical and other scientific research. Modern scientists can be found who will attempt to lay down what 'must' follow for human living from their findings, trying to make 'their' facts into a dominant force. (This is often called 'secularism', the attempt to pervert a positive 'secularization' into an ideology.)

If secularization continues, a Christian can only welcome it. It could be destroyed by warfare; it was severely threatened by Nazism; it is threatened in places like South Africa by racialism, and in many other areas by racialism and nationalism. It is threatened by extreme right- and by extreme left-wing politics. It is threatened by scientism and by indifference. But while it continues, and if it flourishes, it offers immense possibilities for Christian living. Many of the Christian's negative fights are over, struggles to gain freedom 'from' forces that militate against human living and loving. A Christian is much more free to live creatively, rather than defensively; even though the effort may be as great or greater.

It may mean that the Churches will have a chance to make good the harm done in the first two centuries of industrial development. Then a few individual Christians were among those who tried to lessen the hurt of some of the worst symptoms of the industrial disease. But it was left to Engels and Marx to attempt to get to its roots; and a whole urban population grew up outside the Churches. Excessive working hours, a man's selling of his time and energy, his self, as labour, as a unit of production: these are still with us. But technical progress, automation, may finally rid us of them. Then the reward, and the problem, will be leisure. But Christians are much better equipped to interpret the possibilities of leisure. Christian faith, like Jewish faith, is orientated towards relaxation, sabbath, the full life, where nothing that feels like 'work' is done. Relaxation, leisure, as something positive, are a promise that a Christian claims for man in the name of Christ, a promise of fullness and richness in living.[9]

This is not to pretend that it is all obvious. For a variety of reasons, a Christian style of life may seem no real option to a secular man. Christian life is identified for many – Christian and non-Christian alike – with its past battles. Christian Churches find it much easier to go on re-living these past conflicts: it is easiest to fight an enemy that has gone. It is sadly tempting to taunt the champions of secularization into taking the part of the old foes in mock battles, though probably they will refuse to be drawn, and will treat the challenge as an irrelevance.

The Christian foundation documents remain written largely in the terms of the old battles 'against principalities

132

and powers in the heavenly places', and so seem part of the world against which the early Church was fighting. It is time to beat the sword of the ancient warfare into a constructive and creative tool for the present. At least, that is what I would judge that the Spirit whose sword it is, is up to. The construction will be tentative, flexible, open: not the massive fortresses of earlier ages. The Christian will be able to live in love, and freedom and service, more and more fully. He will be alongside Christians and many non-Christians, sharing with them a concern for other people.

## (v) Freedom and the Welfare State

I have listed some largely or quite explicitly Christian voluntary groups where a Christian style of life is being lived. There are still many areas where voluntary and often experimental approaches are appropriate, even essential. But one of the sad things about the Churches is their reluctance to see the areas where once they served and pioneered disappear, or be taken over by professional agencies. It is quite obvious that they have been playing the part of 'benefactors' who use an opportunity for service to lord it over their dependants. This patronizing care seems to have been exercised quite uncritically in the last century. The desperate struggle to cling on to hospitals, schools, youth clubs, and maintain poor ones rather than hand over to the secular state with its much greater financial resources is just a further capitulation to the same temptation. (American objections to 'socialized medicine' may fall in the same category; but they may be as much ideological. And this despite the stress on secular state education in the United States.)

There are still these pioneering Christian and non-Christian agencies and organizations that fill in gaps in present state agencies. And these may well be places where many people will find an authentic Christian freedom for others, a re-living of the life and love of Christ, by the power of the Spirit.

But in a truly secular society, a very high degree of care becomes the right of each citizen that he can demand from statutory bodies. He does not have to depend on his own chance ability and avoidance of calamity; nor on the haphazard availability of ancient trusts or compassionate individuals. The secular state's regard for its own well-being is a very effective factor in making it a 'compassionate society'. (There is a very relevant book of that title by Kathleen Jones, a six-shilling paperback published in 1966 by S.P.C.K. in its 'Here and Now' series.) This creates a situation in which everyone has his area of free choice increased, and people can be related to each other as persons, and not as boss and hand, needy and benefactor, acquisitor and loser.

Admittedly, right-wing politics denies this (sometimes with 'religious' support). It may even be that the most affluent do lose in a modern secular state. But the terms in which the supposed loss is often stated suggest that only the differential has disappeared. In fact, the professor or the director has a greater range of choices than his predecessor; he cannot enjoy them as much for the knowledge that so many of them are now open to his dustman. Certainly the (slow) disappearance of social and – not always linked – accent barriers in Britain enhances freedom and personal life enormously.

Even in an economy that is still massively a free enterprise one, a very large number of people are directly employed by the state, and very largely in 'service' rather than in direct production. It is in this sort of service that Christians will increasingly find their employment and their growth in freedom: in a common concern for persons. This is not without its problems, of course. Welfare services can depersonalize; and they can also cramp and warp where workers insist on inappropriate depths of relationship. A proper respect and reserve are an essential part of concern for persons.

The really critical areas for Christian concern will be in production, where the needs of men and the demands of machines conflict. I may well be wrong in a prediction in this area that is so foreign to me; but my only hope (which is a fairly confident one) is that the problem will be solved by its removal, and that automation will reduce working hours to a point where no one is dominated by greedy machinery.

In a secular age we can look forward to wide areas of choice, rich varieties of leisured culture, more time and opportunity to treat people as people: and so a greatly enhanced possibility of living the freedom offered to us by Jesus the Christ.


## (vi) Freedom and the hungry

My instances so far have been insular and rather domestic. The most chilling threat to all this comes from international tension and the destructive power of modern weapons. But an even deeper threat to the world's enjoyment of secularization is half the world's hunger. If no war comes, but hunger remains, then the promise will have failed. It is the ideological foes of genuine secularization that turn modern resources into weapons, when they could be used to increase food supplies and limit population (preventing conception rather than spreading death). It is here that there are still battles to be won. As yet, here, there are few gains to be consolidated. A Christian can live his freedom only in a concern for others that includes a concern here that he shares deliberately with as many as he can, by voluntary effort that aims at action on a national and international level. A secular age has made this one world, where every major problem is a shared problem. This unity a Christian welcomes, and tries to help to allow it its full positive development.[10]

The diversity of contributory cultures will make a united world still richer than the most fully secular areas themselves yet are. And that will be a basis for Christian living for our great-grandchildren that we can only dream of.

Of course, it could fail. Men are still selfish and short-sighted. There could be almost universal destruction. If there are then Christians among the survivors they will be thrown back on earlier traditions, and battles like the old ones will have to be fought again. But a Christian does not expect disaster, even if he believes he can face it. He trusts a servant Lord, and that this is that Lord's world. Even against the evidence he insists that here and now it is possible to live a love and freedom like that of Jesus; but he expects the evidence to support him.

Where do you find the liberty that is ours as fellow heirs with Christ? In all manner of places, here and now, around us, in the many possibilities of concern with others, for others.

When there are people who share an open active concern for others in our one world, there I would say the life – and death – and resurrection – of Christ is real. I would probably not say it aloud to them, unless I knew them very well. It might seem unreal, antiquated, depriving them of their autonomy. It might seem to them patronizing; or romantic and blind to the failures of which they were well aware. But it would be my belief, and in no ordinary metaphorical way. That for me would be evidence of the life and power of the living Christ, the presence of the Spirit, the love of the Father. For me my belief would enable a more whole-hearted involvement in such a group and its activities. I would expect it so, at least; and that it would be a guard against any self-satisfaction, or any other easy relaxation of concern or betrayal of freedom. Others might have more effective ways, more effective at least for them.

In a group of fellow Christians there would be much more place for an open acknowledgement of the Christ, of the Spirit among us, of the grace of God. But such talk would not necessarily be a large part of our activity. And it would still be tentative and exploratory; in fact a common language for this acknowledgement might be very difficult to find.

The continuing test of the Christ life, the Christian style of life, in a group is the depth of its active common concern for others. The final test comes when it is invited out of an established pattern, however slowly or quickly it had adopted it. When it is asked to accept new members, new functions, new ideas and approaches to the point where it is threatened with death – does it accept death, and the new life that may follow? If it will not allow itself to die, it may still do a great deal of good; but it will lack a distinctive quality of the freedom that was lived by Jesus who died, the God who lived our life.

It is possible to share in a life that is at any rate at many points like the life Jesus lived; you may even find it makes sense to suppose that in some sense there is God who empowers your sharing. You can find this among people committed to him, or people for whom he is not even very interesting. It may well be that in your situation a possibility of this sort is open to you. You have seen it and taken it – or rejected it. If you or I have thought about Jesus at all, then the life you or I lead is the most important thing we have to say about Christology, the doctrine of the Christ. Has he proved God enough to share with us the freedom that was his as a man? The man for us and the God for us? It remains for the jury to give its verdict.

## (vii) The final verdict

Martin has still not had a 'breakdown'. He has had his eyes opened a little by the trial, sees a bit more the relevance of Jesus for living. Left on his own, this will probably gnaw at him, and increase the feelings of guilt he has when things go wrong. He will not manage easily to live up to his intensified ideal. But for the moment, all this talk about 'grace' and 'freedom' and living for others is just talk. He'll go on thinking it is talk, all being well (no, we do *not* want him to have a breakdown), unless he meets up with a group in which the talk is acted out fairly directly. For the time being, his vote is 'against'.

Nesta is horrified. A pattern of belief and action that had seemed plain and straightforward has disappeared before her eyes. For the time being she has 'lost her faith', feels she has been deliberately deceived, and is violently anti-Christian. She has found some consolation in a very high-minded and puritanically rationalist publication. Her reaction is so violent that she may swing back again, if this new way fails her. But it may give her all the support she needs. For the moment, her vote is 'against'.

Tom is still a Marxist. There is no freedom, Jesus'

freedom, or anyone else's, in a capitalist society. But the Chinese cultural revolution has made him more open to a true secularization. Harry does not understand; though he is genuinely pleased that the parson is in favour of the Welfare State and the Labour Party, and he is happy to forgive and forget. Dick has been completely shattered by Austen and Rudi and Jacqueline. They saw straight through him very early on, and were quite unworried. They took him as he stood, and made sure he was part of what was going on. They neither condemned nor condoned. So he is 'for', at least while he is among them.

Austen is impressed with the this-worldly spirituality which seems to be made possible. Much of what the older language said, and that attracted him, is said here; God is even more fully involved in the man Jesus than some classical theology allowed; and so long as the Mass is not too much altered, he is content. And he is fascinated by the others; he has never been brought so inescapably up against other people; and it has been good. His vote remains firmly 'for'.

Gupta has added some more ideas to his already massive store; but the absolute claims, that Jesus is still said to make, offend him, and his vote is 'against'. Jacqueline has found less pain in the jury than she expected, and has not even tried to seduce Dick. With Rudi, Dick, and Austen she has found herself part of something fuller which seems to centre on this man Jesus, but goes out to more than the four of them. Losing yourself this way, it hurts less than in the past to find yourself again. Maybe she can dare to care and love and give herself, not just her sex. Her vote is 'for'.

Of all those who are voting 'against', John is least certain. The jury as a whole had resisted his attempts to dominate it, to capture the attention all the time: but this small group within it had something that might work for him. Only it would not dissociate itself firmly from the rejecting majority. He retains his lonely protesting anger. All this talk of openness and freedom for others is too good to be true. It is too quiet and too trusting. You could lose what you saw was good if you went about it in this way.

Rudi is perhaps happiest with the case for Jesus as it has been presented. This is a real self-giving and a real acceptance by God in Christ, and by Christ in the three others, and in some way by the whole jury. So that leaves it at four to six. You and I, I have said, vote with our lives: the others, being make-believe, can only vote with their opinions. At best it will be a balance. At worst, the majority will be two-to-one against. Still, even with majority verdicts, that is a decision just to ignore him, set him free from changing us, trying to set ourselves free from being judged by him. They cannot kill him a second time. They can only decide to forget him.

The way we live decides the balance. Will he be ignored? Perhaps we may let him still judge us, disturb us, set us free: free to care together for others, and maybe disturb them: share freedom with them, and receive from them his love again.

No? well, he has other advocates.

And even if it works, there is no way of telling that it is 'true'? If you cannot prove it all either true – or false – then is it even meaningful? It is meaningful, in so far as we have seen what it means to live it. And in a practical and technical age 'it works' is pretty fair commendation – if it does. A further sort of proof is offered, but a rather odd sort of proof.

Christians have claimed that the ultimate future belongs to Jesus the Christ. The love that we have glimpsed, the freedom for others that we have begun just to feel, the power of the Spirit that has troubled the surface of our self-concern, this will not die with death. We shall live with him in the perfect love of the undivided triune God into whose life the life of the man Jesus was accepted: the triune God whose love most fully reached us in Jesus and his company of friends.

So we offer a sort of proof, a promise that a proof will be forthcoming. It is an odd proof to offer, because if our prediction is wrong, there will be no one to register its failure. And there is no present proving test for the truth of what is said.[11]

We have to remain satisfied with (or put off by) the question, 'Does it work?' and hope that the life, that we trust is real, will invade our lives now enough to persuade us to live in love, concern, and freedom. The hope will colour our living now, but it is for our living now that we are given it. It is here that we find the people among whom we learn to be loved and to love; and we may find that we can live and spend ourselves, because we trust that the love we give and receive finds its source in a life that is inexhaustible.

If we shall have been wrong, it will have been a good mistake. We leave to Jesus, Son of God, with the Father and the Holy Spirit the last word – or the ultimate silence.

### INTRODUCTION

1 From the 'Definition of Chalcedon', produced by the Council which met there A.D. 451, accepted as authoritative by most of the 'historic' Churches; quoted from *Documents of the Christian Church*, ed. H. Bettenson, 2nd edn (Oxford University Press 1963), p. 73

### CHAPTER I

1 Lord Beaverbrook, *The Divine Propagandist* (Heinemann 1962), p. 29
2 D. H. Lawrence, 'The Man Who Died', pp. 13, 41; in *The Short Novels*, II (Heinemann 1956)
3 George Tyrrell, *Christianity at the Cross-Roads*, 2nd edn (Allen & Unwin 1963), p. 49
4 For the very varied ideas of Jesus that other modern authors have, I suggest this short list. But it could be enlarged very easily to cover an even greater range of disagreements:

    H. Zahrnt, *The Historical Jesus* (Collins 1963)
    James Peter, *Finding the Historical Jesus* (Collins 1965)
    G. Bornkamm, *Jesus of Nazareth* (Hodder & Stoughton 1960)
    H. J. Schonfield, *The Passover Plot* (Hutchinson 1965)
    J. Carmichael, *The Death of Jesus* (Gollancz 1963; Penguin Books 1966)
    J. M. Allegro, *The Dead Sea Scrolls: A Reappraisal*, 2nd edn (Penguin Books 1964) taken with: G. Vermès, *The Dead Sea Scrolls in English* (Penguin Books 1962)
    F. J. Sheed, *To Know Christ Jesus* (Sheed & Ward 1962)
    H. G. Wells, *The Outline of History* (Cassell 1920)
    R. Graves and J. Podro, *The Nazarene Gospel Restored* (Cassell 1953)
    W. N. Pittenger, *The Word Incarnate* (Nisbet 1959)
    R. Bultmann, *Jesus and the Word* (Collins: Fontana Books 1958)
    H. J. Cadbury, *The Peril of Modernizing Jesus* (Macmillan 1937; S.P.C.K. 1962)
    T. R. Glover, *The Jesus of History* (S.C.M. Press 1917)
and in particular, for this book:
    P. M. van Buren, *The Secular Meaning of the Gospel* (S.C.M. Press 1963)
    R. Tennant, *Born of a Woman* (S.P.C.K. 1961)
    Werner and Lotte Pelz, *God Is No More* (Gollancz 1963) and *True Deceivers* (Collins 1966)
    G. Ainger, *Jesus our Contemporary* (S.C.M. Press 1967)
5 Lord Eccles, *Half-way to Faith* (Bles 1966), p. 23

6 Bornkamm, *Jesus of Nazareth*, pp. 9, 22; quoted with approval by H. Zahrnt, *The Historical Jesus*, p. 96

7 Lord Eccles, *Half-way to Faith*, pp. 121, 124

8 Karl Barth, *Church Dogmatics*, I, i; quoted by D. M. Baillie, *God Was in Christ* (Faber 1948), p. 17; Paul Tillich, *Systematic Theology* (Nisbet 1953–55); J. A. T. Robinson, *Honest to God* (S.C.M. Press 1963)

9 see, for instance, Michael Argyle, *Religious Behaviour* (Routledge & Kegan Paul 1958)

10 *A New Reformation?* is the title of a recent book by Bishop Robinson (S.C.M. Press 1965).

11 A good introduction to current technical discussions of Christology is John McIntyre's *The Shape of Christology* (S.C.M. Press 1966). See also N. Pittenger, *The Word Incarnate* and D. M. Baillie, *God Was in Christ*. The first formative centuries are magisterially surveyed in A. Grillmeier, *Christ in Christian Tradition* (Mowbray 1965).

12 Dietrich Bonhoeffer, *Letters and Papers from Prison*, revised edn (S.C.M. Press 1967); also in Collins Fontana Books

CHAPTER 2

1 On this, see Michael Polanyi, *Personal Knowledge* (Routledge & Kegan Paul 1958); J. S. Habgood, *Religion and Science* (Mills & Boon 1964)

2 see Zahrnt, op. cit.; also a book which I hope to publish under some such title as *A Quest for Jesus and the Early Church*; see also J. L. Austin, 'Unfair to Facts', in *Philosophical Papers*, ed. J. O. Urmson and G. J. Warnock (Oxford University Press 1961) and E. H. Carr, *What is History?* (Penguin Books 1964)

3 John 9: 39; see commentaries on this theme

4 These characters have *some* relationship to outstanding theological figures; but that is not at all necessary to understand what I am saying. I leave it for those who care to amuse themselves that way to puzzle it out. The punning names are part-clues.

5 The traditional words in hymns and prayer books and sermons are 'satisfaction', 'propitiation', 'atonement'. In feudal days, a sin seemed to wound God's honour, which had to be 'satisfied'; in more personal terms, God seemed wrathful, and had to be 'propitiated', appeased; in terms of commerce and the law courts, punishment must be suffered to 'atone' for law-breaking, or a debt of sin must be paid off by someone, it does not matter much by whom, so long as they have the wherewithal.

6 To be fair, Tom could read this in exactly the opposite way: to elect Jesus to an equal partnership *may* be an attempt to infiltrate the heavenly establishment, subvert it by a palace revolution. When this election was being most hotly debated, in the 4th century A.D., those most opposed to Jesus' promotion wanted him as

Works Manager, definitely subordinate in the total scheme of things. (These were the 'Arians', led by one Arius. Their views are shared today by Jehovah's Witnesses.) But Tom is right, there are more ways of getting rid of a trouble-maker than sacking him. The Roman Empire gave up the attempt to suppress Jesus, and did their best to take him on. They were very interested in getting what was, in their political terms, 'the best answer' accepted.

7 In fact, in another tradition, Austen could have used the ideas that are labelled 'from Antioch' to obtain an understanding of Jesus and God that would make sense to him. I have already mentioned that some writers talk of Jesus being completely 'transparent' to God: Jesus' individuality disappears, and he points wholly to God. He obeys so fully that he has no independent existence; through him you are presented with the fullness of God, God reveals himself to your obedient contemplation and service. You are lost in the awed delight of seeing more and more fully the intellectual implications of this idea of God's self-revelation. It is not as thorough-going as Alexandria can be; but it can still make good sense to a man like Austen.

8 There are, of course, more forms of retreat from individual and inter-personal life. Some let you believe in God who is the mirror of your 'real' self beyond the physical, hurtful world around – a mirror of yourself into which you may merge. For others God may be the Other who threatens to prevent you from ceasing to be, who presents himself to you as the one who will wake you if ever you seem likely to fall into the womb-tight sleep you long for. Or he is the image of yourself that you wish to destroy, and just cannot trust.

At least one philosopher (from memory, Antony Flew) has said that his atheism is only Protestantism carried to its logical conclusion – the God who is pushed further and further from the unacceptable world around, until he is so far 'beyond being' and 'beyond personality' that he is not: even if you have to go on proving his absence more busily than his believers need to show he is there.

And the theologian who uses sophisticated language may seem 'advanced'; but it could be that he is further in retreat from adult reality than is his traditionalist friend who talks to 'Daddy out there' – the former can be a retreat back 'beyond personality' to the death-sleep of the womb. (See my review/article in *The Honest to God Debate*, ed. David L. Edwards, S.C.M. Press 1963.)

Types of theism, atheism, agnosticism may each be powerfully attractive to different people for very similar psychological reasons. That tells you little about any ultimate 'truth' in each position. It just tells you quite a lot about the attractiveness to or repulsion from the case you are making felt by any person or group. Or about your own reactions to this book's case: for or against.

CHAPTER 3

1 For what follows, see, for instance, the books by G. Bornkamm, H. Zahrnt, P. M. van Buren, R. Tennant, W. and L. Pelz, referred to on page 142, Chapter 1, note 4; and to the forthcoming book on this topic that I hope to produce.

2 Mark 2:13ff.

3 e.g. Mark 10:17–31

4 e.g. Matthew 18:21–35

5 Mark 9:33–37; 10:13–16; Matthew 11:16–19

6 see the material preserved in Matthew 5–7; Mark 8:34ff.

7 Mark 12:28–34; 1:4–11; Luke 7:18–35; Mark 10:17ff.; Luke 10:25–37; Matthew 25:31–46; Luke 16:1–8; Matthew 13:44,45

8 Mark 12; Luke 15

9 Mark 10:32–end of the gospel; and the other Passion Narratives

10 John 8:1–11 (accepting this as good tradition); Luke 7:36–50

11 e.g. Mark 5:34

12 Mark 2:17; Luke 18:9–14

13 Mark 4; Matthew 13; Luke 7, etc.

15 Luke 11:1–13

14 Luke 11:2; Mark 14:36ff.

16 Mark 1:14f.; 10:35–45; Luke 22:24–30 (John 13)

17 Mark 10:17; 2:1–12; 4; Luke 15:11–32; Matthew 8:11

18 Luke 18:9–14; 17:7–9; Matthew 20:1–15

19 Matthew 6:19–34; 12:25–29

20 Matthew 5:1–12, 38–48

21 Mark 10:1–12

22 There is no proof that any of the preceding material refers in fact to 'Jesus as he was'; but there could not be proof, anyway. None (or very little) is at all obviously purely a product of the later Church(es). This can be taken only as a sign of how little we know of the later community(-ies). It is bound to be arbitrary, but it is reasonably arbitrary. Reasoning wilfulness is the essence of historical reconstruction. As I have already said a number of times, I hope in due course to defend this more fully.

23 For a discussion of the titles of Jesus, see R. H. Fuller, *The Foundations of New Testament Christology* (Lutterworth Press 1965). That he used the term 'Son of Man' of himself is defended (for differing senses of the term) by E. Schweizer, *Lordship and Discipleship* (S.C.M. Press 1960); art. 'The Son of

Man again', in *Journal of New Testament Studies* **9** (1963); also see A. J. B. Higgins, *Jesus and the Son of Man* (Lutterworth Press 1964)

[24] see an article by my brother, J. Downing, 'Jesus and Martyrdom', in *Journal of Theological Studies*, new series, xiv, 2 (October 1963)

[25] see his letter to Christians in Galatia

CHAPTER 4

[1] This chapter is based on a Compline address given at Lincoln Theological College, and a broadcast talk on the BBC Third Programme, on 25 December 1964, entitled 'The Logic of Love'.

[2] For a picture of 'philosophical analysis' and its implications for Christian faith, see Frederick Ferré, *Language, Logic and God* (Eyre & Spottiswoode 1962); the second half of my own *Has Christianity a Revelation?* (S.C.M. Press 1964), and books listed there; especially D. D. Evans, *The Logic of Self-Involvement* (S.C.M. Press 1963). The topic is discussed further in the next chapter.

[3] Philippians 2:5ff.

[4] 1 John 4:10; 1 Corinthians 15:10; Romans 7:24f.

[5] This trust in the attractiveness of Jesus is most powerfully conveyed in the writings of W. and L. Pelz, quoted in Chapter 1, note 4; see also P. M. van Buren and R. Tennant. 'Sharing Jesus' freedom' is a particularly important theme in van Buren.

[6] The phrase ' "throw themselves away" on each other', of the marriage relationship, is Dr Eric Mascall's. And on this section, see especially N. W. Clerk (pseudonym of C. S. Lewis), *A Grief Observed* (Faber 1961).

[7] Pascal's wager is described, disapprovingly, in John Hick, *Philosophy of Religion* (Prentice-Hall 1963), p. 64f. See *Pascal's Pensées*, Everyman's Library (Dent 1932), p. 67

[8] This I anticipated above, in note 8 to Chapter 3. The 'abstract' language that I am discussing occurs particularly in Paul Tillich and his followers (e.g. J. A. T. Robinson, in *Honest to God*); but not exclusively there. See *The Honest to God Debate*, ed. David L. Edwards (S.C.M. Press 1963)

[9] for instance, Pittenger, *The Word Incarnate*

[10] I refer to my *Has Christianity a Revelation?*

[11] Something of this is also said in H. Montefiore, *Awkward Questions on Christian Love* (Collins Fontana Books 1964).

[12] An 'extreme' Alexandrian type of view is supported by Dr Eric Mascall in, for example, *Christ, the Christian and the Church* (Longmans 1946). My own view is probably nearest to that of L. Hodgson in, for example, *And Was Made Man* (Longmans 1928).

[13] There is an impressive essay by Karl Barth in a collection to which it gives the title, *The Humanity of God*, though Barth does not (need I say, 'of course'?) make the further deductions that I do. This is technically, at least superficially, like a 'kenotic' or 'emptying' Christology: God is said to 'empty himself' of some of his attributes – omniscience, omnipotence, omnipresence – to become man. And then it is 'not really God'. It makes more sense, on a Christian basis, to suppose that God is always able to do just this,

and does not become less God for doing so. See O. C. Quick, *Doctrines of the Creed* (Nisbet 1938), chapter XIII, esp. pp. 125, 135; also P. M. van Buren, *Christ in our Place* (Oliver & Boyd 1957): 'Is not this the glory of God, so different from human conceptions of glory, that He can abandon His own glory?' (p. 13 and *passim*)

This, of course, raises the whole question of the 'possibility' of God. Traditionally, God is said to be 'impassible'. That is mainly intended to ensure that we do not suppose that we can sway God, twist him to our whims; or suppose that he is fickle. But it seems to say that God cannot be affected by anything; and that would mean, cannot love in any meaningful sense of 'love'. As Pascal insisted, this God of the philosophers is not the God of Abraham, Isaac, or Jacob; nor is he the God of Paul or of ordinary Christian devotion. See further D. L. Edwards, *God's Cross in our World* (S.C.M. Press 1963), p. 113f.; Kazoh Kitamori, *Theology of the Pain of God* (S.C.M. Press 1966); K. J. Woollcombe, 'The Pain of God', in *Scottish Journal of Theology*, xx, 2 (June 1967), for a very carefully qualified refusal to be bound by the '*apathes*' tradition.

14 'The paradox of grace' is a key phrase in D. M. Baillie's *God Was in Christ*; it is taken up and elaborated by N. Pittenger. See my *Has Christiantity a Revelation?*, pp. 261–274

15 For talk about 'The Trinity' that fits more or less with what is said here, see L. Hodgson, *The Doctrine of the Trinity* (Nisbet 1943); *For Faith and Freedom*, ii (Blackwell 1957), p. 225ff.; also J. McIntyre, *On the Love of God* (Collins 1962)

16 A. J. Ayer, I notice, discusses in an essay the question of identity, and the meaning-fulness of talk of sharing identity; his conclusions seem to me to justify my basic approach; though (again, need I say, 'of course'?) he does not intend this sort of application of his analysis. See his *The Concept of a Person and other Essays* (Macmillan 1963)

17 Christina Rossetti, 'In the bleak mid-winter'

18 'My God, I love thee; not because', from a 17th-century Latin translation of a Spanish sonnet (attributed to St Francis Xavier)

### CHAPTER 5

1 On the picture of science, see J. S. Habgood, *Religion and Science* (Mills & Boon 1964); Michael Polanyi, *Personal Knowledge* (Routledge & Kegan Paul 1958); also James A. Coleman, *Relativity for the Layman* (Macmillan, New York 1959: Penguin Books 1964); Banesh Hoffmann, *The Strange Story of the Quantum* (Penguin Books 1963); J. W. Lewis, in *Faith, Fact and Fantasy* (Collins 1964)

2 For the philosophers, see the books quoted above; also, for instance, J. O. Urmson, *Philosophical Analysis* (Oxford University Press 1956). For the effects of 'science', and the philosophy that goes hand in hand with it, on

theological discourse and thinking, see many of note 1; and, for instance, T. R. Miles, *Religion and the Scientific Outlook* (Allen & Unwin 1959)

3 For the term 'model' in this sort of context, see Ian T. Ramsey, *Models and Mystery* (Oxford University Press 1964) and other of his writings. The distinctions I draw between 'meaning' and 'working' models is, however, determined by a certain amount of disagreement that I have with Dr Ramsey. He talks about models for 'discernment situations'; to me these are much less important. This terminology is also used by J. McIntyre in *The Shape of Christology*, which I have referred to. I recommend it as a useful book; with the one qualification that I find its use of 'model' language confusing.

4 This is what I was saying in the previous chapter. See also my *Has Christianity a Revelation?*, chapter 5

5 For 'is' and 'ought', see R. M. Hare, *The Language of Morals* (Oxford University Press 1952) and *Freedom and Reason* (Oxford University Press 1963)

6 For this necessary connexion after the essential analysis, see the above books; and also J. L. Austin, *How to Do Things with Words* (Oxford University Press 1962); and D. D. Evans, *The Logic of Self-Involvement*

7 For a critical discussion of the proofs, together with an insistence that they are important for Christians – and invalid – see A. Flew, *God and Philosophy* (Hutchinson 1966). For other interpretations, see Sidney Hook (ed.), *Religious Experience and Truth* (Oliver & Boyd 1962), various essays; also many of the contributions to the Australian journal, *Sophia*

8 David Jenkins, *The Glory of Man* (S.C.M. Press 1967), p. 2f.

9 A. J. Heschel, *Who is Man?* (Oxford University Press 1966), p. 11 and *passim*

10 For this, see my *Has Christianity a Revelation?*, esp. p. 286ff.; also W. and L. Pelz, *God Is No More*; N. W. Clerk, *A Grief Observed*; D. M. MacKinnon, in *Objections to Christian Belief*, ed. A. R. Vidler (Constable 1963), p. 31ff.

11 see Fr Rodzianko, in *Theology*, February 1964

CHAPTER 6

1 This section of this book is also based on Compline addresses at Lincoln Theological College. On Determinism, see Hoffmann, *The Strange Story of the Quantum*; also essays in *Determinism and Freedom in the Age of Modern Science*, ed. S. Hook (Collier, New York 1961); and Ian T. Ramsey, *Freedom and Immortality* (S.C.M. Press 1960) on Heisenberg (p. 18)

2 The theme of 'freedom for the future' and 'from the past' is dealt with powerfully in the writings of Rudolf Bultmann; also by W. and L. Pelz.

3 D. Jenkins, *The Glory of Man*, chapters III and IV

4 see Albert H. van den Heuvel, *These Rebellious Powers* (S.C.M. Press 1966)

5 Galatians 3–5; esp. 5:13

6 Galatians 3:28

7 Elisabeth Adler (ed.), '*Pro-Existence*' (S.C.M. Press 1964)

8 see Edward Rogers, *Living Standards* (S.C.M. Press 1964); R. H. Fuller and B. Rice, *Christianity and the Affluent Society* (Hodder & Stoughton 1966);

also the Report of the British Council of Churches, *World Poverty and British Responsibility*, revised and enlarged edn (S.C.M. Press 1967)

9 E. M. Forster, in *A Passage to India*, has a character speak of 'poor little talkative Christianity'. I realize that I have not explicitly said in the text what I strongly feel about Christian religious talk, proclamation, chatter. If what I have said about the uncertainty of the Christian's position, and his need to live with uncertainty, is accepted, then it follows that he will maintain a considerable reserve. He will be very slow to talk to non-Christians about his faith. He will no longer suppose that sermons or books about his beliefs are a great gift to the world at large. He will accept that he has no 'revelation' to offer. He can just live his faith, accept and give friendship, share common interests.

This may or may not raise questions in other people's minds. 'By your fruits they will know you.' If questions come – explicit, or tentative but real – then and then only will you speak about what you believe. For that opportunity you will be as prepared and as open as possible.

I do not expect the words of this book to persuade an 'unbeliever' (even if such a person ever sets eyes on them). They are meant to help us believers to make our faith articulate to ourselves (and this *is* an urgent obligation), so that perhaps we may live our commitment that much more fully. And if they do, they may help in talking to someone whose interest has been aroused by his contact with you or some other Christians. ' . . . our traditional language must perforce become powerless and remain silent, and our Christianity to-day will be confined to praying for and doing right by our fellow men.' (Dietrich Bonhoeffer, *Letters and Papers from Prison*, 2nd edn, S.C.M. Press 1956, p. 140)

CHAPTER 7

1 Some books on group relations:
> R. D. Laing, *The Divided Self* (Tavistock Publications 1960; Penguin Books 1965); *The Self and Others* (Tavistock Publications 1961); *The Politics of Experience* (Penguin Books 1967)
> J. A. C. Brown, *The Social Psychology of Industry* (Penguin Books 1954)
> W. H. J. Sprott, *Human Groups* (Penguin Books 1958)
> M. Argyle, *The Psychology of Interpersonal Behaviour* (Penguin Books 1967)
> E. Berne, *The Structure and Dynamics of Organizations and Groups* (Lippincott, Philadelphia 1963)
> D. Cartwright and A. Zander (eds), *Group Dynamics* (Row, Peterson & Co., Evanston 1953; Tavistock Publications 1960)

2 The contemporary American theologian, John Knox, has written a book called *The Church and the Reality of Christ* (Collins 1963). In it he accepts a lot of the most radical historical criticism (he is a leading New Testament scholar). He suggests, against this background, that, apart from the Church which preserves the 'memory' of Jesus the Christ, there is no Christ. If there is a saving (or revealing) event, act of God, it is the life and death of Christ together with, inseparable from, the coming to life of the Church which then continued down the centuries. Knox very carefully refuses to be romantic or hazily mystical about this 'Church'; and refuses to be over-dogmatic, either. I find his position very attractive, and it has influenced what I say in this book. None the less, I am more committed to the figure of the historic Jesus (however uncertain any picture of him must be) and less committed to the historic Church (especially if that be taken to mean the self-preserving traditional institution). The life of Christ is real, in some way that makes a difference to us, only where people are actively committed to him, or to aims that overlap with his. But, as I have said, from that I come to believe in his present reality, standing over against me and any 'Church', old or new.

3 On the Holy Spirit, see F. A. Cockin, *God in Action* (Penguin Books 1961); Romans 5:5; 2 Corinthians 3:17

4 see Kathleen Jones, *The Compassionate Society* (S.P.C.K. 1966), chapter IV; Ernest Southcott, *The Parish Comes Alive* (Mowbray 1956); *Layman's Church*, ed. T. Beaumont (Lutterworth Press 1963), esp. the essay by Mark Gibbs; Colin Williams, *Where in the World?* (Epworth Press 1965); many of the contributions to *Planning for Mission*, ed. T. Wieser (Epworth Press 1966) – the phrase used is 'teamwork'; Kathleen Bliss, *We the People* (S.C.M. Press 1963), final chapter

5 Christianity and 'the arts': K. M. Baxter, *Speak What We Feel* (S.C.M. Press 1964); Valerie Pitt, *The Writer and the Modern World* (S.P.C.K. 1966); A. C. Bridge, *Images of God* (Hodder & Stoughton 1960); D. Whittle, *Christianity and the Arts* (Mowbray 1966)

6 see N. W. Clerk, *A Grief Observed*; William Hamilton, *The New Essence of Christianity* (Darton, Longman & Todd 1966)

7 Compare the Dutch Roman Catholic, Robert Adolfs, *The Grave of God* (Burns and Oates 1967)

8 Other works on the theme of 'the secular': Colin Williams, *Faith in a Secular Age* (Collins Fontana Books 1966); *On the Battle Lines*, ed. Malcolm Boyd (S.C.M. Press 1964); van den Heuvel, *These Rebellious Powers*; T. W. Ogletree, *The 'Death of God' Controversy* (S.C.M. Press 1966); Lesslie Newbigin, *Honest Religion for Secular Man* (S.C.M. Press 1966): one of the

more 'conservative' positive appreciations; very much opposed: E. L. Mascall, *The Secularisation of Christianity* (Darton, Longmann & Todd 1965)

[9] see, for instance, E. R. Wickham, *Church and People in an Industrial City* (Lutterworth Press 1957); also his *Encounter with Modern Society* (Lutterworth Press 1964)

[10] see the books by Rogers and by Fuller and Rice, mentioned previously, Chapter 6, note 8

[11] see John Hick, *Philosophy of Religion*, p. 100ff.; *Evil and the God of Love* (Macmillan 1966), esp. p. 17

# Index

Subjects and authors in the Notes are not entered in the Index. Biblical references also are listed only in the Notes.